THE ACQUISITION OF THE HOLY SPIRIT
VOL. I

The Acquisition of the Holy Spirit in Russia
SERIES

PROFESSOR I. M. KONTZEVITCH AND HIS WIFE HELEN
in front of their icon corner, at the time they collaborated
on this book. Paris, 1950.

THE ACQUISITION OF THE HOLY SPIRIT

ORTHODOX ASCETIC THEOLOGY
Vol. I

by I. M. Kontzevitch

ST. HERMAN OF ALASKA BROTHERHOOD
1996

Address all correspondence to:
St. Herman of Alaska Brotherhood
P.O. Box 70
Platina, California 96076

Cover: Greek icon showing All Saints—Acquirers of the Holy Spirit.

Library of Congress Cataloging in Publication Data

Kontzevitch, I. M., 1893-1965.
    The acquisition of the Holy Spirit in ancient Russia.
    1. Christianity — Eastern Orthodox Spirituality. 2. History — Byzantine
and Russian. 3. Russia — Church History.
    I. Title.
Library of Congress Catalogue Number 88-063597
ISBN 0-938635-73-5

The author dedicates this book
to the light-bearing memory of his mother,
Nun Nectaria.

The translator dedicates this edition
to the memory of her parents,
John and Evdokia.

The publishers dedicate this book
to the Millennium of Holy Russia.

CONTENTS

EDITOR'S PREFACE

I.

HE ACQUISITION OF THE HOLY SPIRIT is the main aim of man upon this earth, for it is through the ascetic struggle of "pulling down" the Holy Spirit into a repentant, humble heart that man gains justification before the face of God. Christ is our Savior only as long as we realize we are perishing; and the acquisition of the Holy Spirit is the actuality of being saved.

When Our Lord Jesus Christ sent down the Holy Spirit as He promised to His faithful followers, it was the personal, individual exploit of people of various nationalities that, having led to the saving state of union with God, transformed whole nations. Having the original apostolic community as a model, countries have built their civilizations on Christian principles, on the Faith of Christ that makes man Godlike. At various stages in the history of Western civilization, Christianity has made inroads and created saints who have become national heroes; and these heroes have set the tone for the specific characteristics of their respective nations. In one way or another these nations, becoming infused with holiness, have developed indigenous qualities of sanctity which have colored the essence of their arts, literature and customs.

Christian ethnic characteristics are valid only if they stem from the genuine acquisition of the Holy Spirit. This unites all in Christ, and thus to the state of Adam before the Fall, to the paradisiacal state for which man was made. But if there is no link and there is estrangement from that initial source — the traditional, historical path of acquiring the Holy Spirit — then the result is separation, peculiarity and oddity, a source of strife and discord. The historical acquisition of the Holy Spirit as reflected in local, national churches has created a heavenly choir composed of earthly men and women who have transfigured themselves into saints — friends of God.

11

The path to acquire the state of sanctity is not an easy one because it involves the voluntary self-crucifixion of the fallen man — and war with the devil, the flesh and the world. But for today's God-thirsting neophytes, this 2,000 year-old path has certainly been well-trodden, cleared and sign-posted with knowledge that has been acquired from practice and passed down in the context of various languages and cultures by God-loving pastors and teachers who have known God first-hand. Such knowledge constitutes Patristic Theology, the ascetic or practical aspect of which has been well presented by I. M. Kontzevitch in his work, *The Acquisition of the Holy Spirit in Ancient Russia.* This book, which is presented here for the first time in the English language, is the result of the independent will of a loving scholar who encountered a saint in his youth, St. Nectarius of Optina. Impressed by the reality of sanctity being alive in the 20th century, Kontzevitch dedicated his whole life to preserving and presenting the path to this sanctity, the guides or directors of which were holy elders unknown to Western Christendom.

II.

To commemorate a thousand years of Christianity in Russia, we present to the contemporary reader a series of modern patristic texts hitherto unpublished in the English language. Even in modern times, with the revival of Orthodox Christian values, Russia has produced an amazing output of sanctity, firmly rooted in and stemming from ancient Byzantium. Such phenomenal wellsprings of spirituality as Sts. Seraphim of Sarov, John of Kronstadt, Paisius Velichkovsky and his Optina disciples, the New Martyrs of Russia, and the Blessed Wonderworker John Maximovitch — are all universal gifts bequeathed from the Holy Russia of modern times. These Saints, as well as the Orthodox ascetic theology which made them such, have not been presented adequately for contemporary men and women. It was the hope of our late Professor Kontzevitch to acquaint contemporary God-seekers with the very essence of the Orthodox hagiographical tradition — the acquisition of the Holy Spirit as a manifestation of the Apostolic offices of saints and prophets.

As the first volume in this series, *The Acquisition of the Holy Spirit* strives to give a historic survey of the very nature of sanctity as it has been revealed historically and acquired by genuine carriers of grace. This, the main work of Professor Kontzevitch, gives a 1,000-year panorama of historic climates and conditions which were either conducive or hostile to the spread of the God-chosen men and women, called God-bearing Fathers and Mothers by the Orthodox Church.

The book is divided into two subjects: 1) what in essence is basic Christian asceticism, and 2) how it originated and spread to Russia. The authors, Ivan and his wife Helen Kontzevitch, were living representatives of that very tradition that produced saints: they were linked to St. Seraphim, St. John of Kronstadt, the Optina Elders, and more recent saints and martyrs who have adorned the "Church Triumphant" in heaven. A brief biography of the author and his wife are to be found in the Appendix, which deliberately mentions righteous men and women bound up with them, hitherto unknown, who would have remained in oblivion.

This book, written under very unfavorable post-war conditions, is essentially a textbook of ascetic theology. This is a subject that has been neglected in contemporary theological schools, resulting in the apparent lack of sanctity in today's Orthodox society. The aim of the authors and the publisher is to fill this gap — to inspire Orthodox Christians to lead a true spiritual Orthodox life in conjunction with the spread of Orthodox revival, both in the Free World and behind the Iron Curtain. By publishing this work, we realize that the book will reach Russia, be re-translated and do its work toward the salvation of many souls.

The value of this work lies not only in its exposition of the very essence of Christian religion, so meticulously and precisely presented, but also in the fact that the authors had direct contact with saints who themselves acquired the Holy Spirit. It is not only a scholarly study, abundant in research and data, but is in itself almost a personal testimony by the authors, concealed in their humbleness.

A few points are not sufficiently developed in the book: first, the "Viking influence" coming upon ancient Russia by way of the Northwest, from which came Olga, the grandmother of St. Vladimir the evangelizer; and, secondly, the influence of Valaam Monastery, which through Sts. Abramius and Leontius of Rostov influenced the great St. Sergius of Radonezh, the Abba of all North Russian monks.

The women saints are almost omitted, but an appendix was written twenty years later with the participation of the author's wife. A whole series of saints, namely those of the Kiev caves, were skimmed over because of the lack of time and space. Moreover, the ending of the book was not fully finished. It is hoped that the special sections on iconography and the Orthodox philosophy of Kireyevsky will supplement the apparent gap.

In addition to brief biographies of modern Russian ascetics, a whole series of monographs on the Optina Elders are intended to follow in this series, so as to complete the picture of the attempted Triology of Professor Kontzevitch. *The Acquisition of the Holy Spirit* was to be Volume I; a book on the immediate disciples of St. Paisius Velichkovsky was to be Volume II; and *Optina Monastery and its Era* was to be Volume III. The first came out in 1952, and the third came out twenty years later, briefly incorporating Volume II in its original chapters. The publisher, St. Herman Press, which was founded with Professor Kontzevitch's participation, published in Russian the *prima vitas* of eight major Optina Elders, photographically reproduced from books of the Kontzevitchs' collection; while the Lives of the last two Elders, Barsanuphius and Nectarius, were fully incorporated into *Optina Monastery and its Era*. With God's help and the prayers of our readers, it is hoped that the treasury of these ten volumes will see light in English translations, which have been undertaken with the participation of Professor Ivan Kontzevitch's widow herself.

This, in total, constitutes a spiritual offering to contemporary God-seekers who long to possess not only scholarly editions, but texts which transmit the essence of contemporary ascetic theologians themselves.

III.

Through a reading of *The Acquisition of the Holy Spirit,* many questions and doubts of new converts to Orthodox Christianity will be answered. This book is published in the hope that it will enable readers to refine their power of discernment, which is so imperative today when superficiality and imitation are so rampant. The English-speaking world, although rooted in the Christian understanding of the Holy Spirit being present on earth, is rapidly losing this fine, mathematical precision in identifying the genuine from the seeming. It is hoped that the reader will hesitate a moment before the holy realm contained in this book,·and will call the Holy Spirit to his aid. In such a way will he benefit from this labor of love, and from its pages will come forth hundreds of ascetics whose names are charged with holiness. May those of the English-speaking world not miss the fine line between the state of sanctity and the state of delusion, and may they come out as victors in the lofty activity of acquiring the Holy Spirit. For after all, the intent of the author and publishers is not merely to inform, but to witness to the Divine Fire that historically *did* descend upon this earth, *did* touch the thirsty hearts of fallen men, *did* change the face of whole nations, and *did* deposit into the holy Orthodox tradition a living spark that is alive today and is potent to renew this very English-speaking civilization, causing goodness to spill out even upon unsuspecting bystanders.

Glory be to God for all things!   Abbot Herman
                                                                    October, 1988

PREFACE TO THE
ENGLISH EDITION

HE ACQUISITION OF THE HOLY SPIRIT IN ANCIENT RUSSIA came forth into the world in Paris in 1952. A second edition was published in Canada in 1973 by offset, without any changes or corrections. The book is dedicated to the investigation of the spiritual life of the Russian people from the days of Russia's baptism, and especially at the end of the Tatar invasion, when there arose the possibility of having intercommunion with countries of the Near East (Greece, Bulgaria, Serbia) which had assimilated the teaching of St. Gregory Palamas.[1] The crowds of Russian pilgrims who visited these lands, upon their return home, hastened to institute this teaching on their native soil.

By this time St. Sergius of Radonezh erected a monastery in the dense forest in the vicinity of Moscow. This monastery grew to become a spiritual center for the whole land, under the name of Holy Trinity-St. Sergius Lavra. The *Life* of St. Sergius indicates that in his monastery there existed the distinct characteristics of hesychasm, which subsequently affected all ascetic exploits in the northern part of Russia known as the "Northern Thebaid." Amidst fierce northern nature, the life of the ascetics demanded supernatural *podvig*, accompanied by the ceaseless doing of the Jesus Prayer. This Prayer stood as the eternal foundation of the legacy of Russian monastic exploit for the duration of Russian history. In spite of periodic persecutions, hesychasm remained as an inalienable quality of Russian monastic sanctity. Thus it was until the last Elder of Optina Monastery.

---

1. *I.e.*, the teaching of hesychasm. See Part II, chapter 3 *(editor)*.

Closely linked with the tradition of hesychasm is that of eldership. The Apostle Paul talks about gifts, one of which is prophecy (Eph. 4:11). *Eldership is this gift of prophecy.* This idea was not in the Russian editions of *Acquisition,* for we had not arrived at it then. It is now installed in the English edition. In the discovery of this idea lies the whole meaning of the life of Ivan Michailovitch Kontzevitch. It is indeed a discovery, for by it the essence of eldership has been unlocked. Eldership is one of the gifts of the Holy Spirit, which no one understands.

According to the word of St. Paul, *God hath set some in the church, first apostles, secondarily prophets, thirdly teachers, after that miracles, then gifts of healing, helps, governments, diversities of tongues* (I Cor. 12:28). This apostolic decree is unwavering and unchangeable in the entire life of the Church, from the beginning to the end of the ages. It refers first of all to apostolic ministry, in other words, the sanctifying service of the Church. This ministry of service is apparent for all to see. The second ministry is prophetic, and has also been permanently instituted by the Apostle. Although it does not have visual demarcations, it nevertheless has just as inviolable a place in the Church and a firm foundation in ecclesiastical life. The prophets, under the name of eldership, always existed in the Church. The gift of eldership was acquired in asceticism and bound up with monasticism.

Like the teaching of hesychasm, eldership was brought to Russia by pilgrims from the Orthodox East, and from its influence arose the monastery of St. Sergius and the whole of Northern Russian monasticsm. The elders were not tied to the existing order of government, and were therefore free. This is the root of the unofficial Church of the people, which existed during all the days of Russian history. Periodically it endured conflicts with the official Synodal church. At the decline of piety in the country, the elders, bearers of the gift of prophecy, were misunderstood and persecuted. There were many examples of this in the lives of the elders of Optina Monastery. The church authorities wanted to banish Elder Leonid to prison in Solovki. A bishop wanted to expel Elder Ambrose from Shamordino Monastery, and when he came to execute this plan he found the Elder dead. Elder Hieromonk Barsanuphius was forcibly removed from Optina; and the last Elder of Optina, Schemamonk Nectarius, endured a similar fate. Also, the Russian church authorities did not treasure the prophet St. John of Kronstadt. He, too, was subjected to attacks.

Finally, in connection with eldership, it is imperative to say that true monasticism cannot be bound up with pseudo-eldership, the characteristics of which are described in Part I of this book.

Helen Kontzevitch
Berkeley, California

GLOSSARY

akathist: a special, lively service to Jesus Christ, the Mother of God, or a saint, during which one should stand; literally, "not sitting."

antimens (antimension): a shroud in which are sewn the relics of a martyr, and on which a priest serves the Liturgy.

byt: way of life.

chiliasm: specifically, a heresy that asserts that Christ will set up an earthly kingdom; in general, any mentality that expects heavenly blessedness to be realized in any earthly way.

hesychasm: an ascetic practice associated with the anchoretic way of life and involving mental stillness, inner spiritual concentration and unceasing prayer.

hesychast: one who practices mental stillness.

hieromonk: a monk in priestly rank.

kenosis: compassionate self-emptying.

klobuk: monastic headwear.

lavra: a large coenobitic monastery.

metochion (metochia pl., *podvorye* in Russian): a monastic dependency of a large monastery.

moleben: a service for the living.

podvig: ascetic exploit; spiritual struggle.

prelest: spiritual deception or delusion; not seeing reality the way it is.

prosphora: leavened bread for use in the Divine Liturgy.

schemamonk: one who has taken on the highest and strictest monastic discipline, denoted by a special cowl and stole.

semantron: a special board which one hits with a stick in order to call monks to prayer.

skete: a small monastery, usually a close-knit "family" of up to 12 monks with the abbot as their father.

sotainnik: sharer of the monastic secret or mystery *(taina)*; co-mystic.

starchestvo: eldership.

staretz: an elder.

stichera: a verse of liturgical poetry.

OPTINA MONASTERY ON THE ZHIZDRA RIVER

From the Kontzevitch photograph collection.

INTRODUCTION

BY THE AUTHOR

*The stone which the builders rejected
is become the head of the corner.*
(Psalm 117:22)

HE GREATEST GIFT bestowed upon man is his inherent ability for communion with God, for beholding God. In this lies supreme happiness. It is man's task to develop this gift within himself. God's purpose with regard to man is deification.

In "the acquisition of the Holy Spirit" lies the entire meaning of ascetic labors and of the lofty spiritual "mental prayer of the heart." However, if lofty spiritual contemplation here on earth is the lot of the few, unceasing prayer is the duty of every Christian. *In everything give thanks: for this is the will of God in Christ Jesus concerning you* (I Thes. 5:17-18), says the Apostle Paul to Christians, and the great hesychast (man of stillness) St. Gregory Palamas (14th century), calls on everyone to pray unceasingly. According to him, all Christians, not only monks and hermits but laymen as well, should practice unceasing prayer.

The purpose of the first, theoretical part of the present work is to present a comprehensive, if only brief, exposition of the essence of ascetic sobriety and spiritual prayer leading to communion with God and, in connection with this labor *(podvig)*, of grace-giving spiritual counselling as exercised by elders *(startsy)* as a guiding principle. The influence of eldership *(starchestvo)*, how-

19

ever, is not confined within monastery walls: it extends far beyond their borders. Being a guiding principle in the spiritual and moral manifestations of life not only of monastics but also of lay people, it embraces all manifestations of life in general, both spiritual and secular, which are inseparably interconnected and at the same time clearly differentiated.

The second, historical part explores the development of ascetic labors in ancient monasticism in the East and in Russia in the 10th-17th centuries. There is also discussion of the effect of the life-giving forces on the "ways of ancient Russia," when in the days of the early flowering of Christianity they penetrated to the depth of the nation's heart.

The author's initial inspiration for the present work came about as a desire to systematize the uncoordinated printed material dealing with the Lives of the last Elders of Optina — namely, the Lives of Schema-archimandrite Barsanuphius and Hiero-schemamonk Nectarius — and to convey his personal reminiscences of visits to the Optina Monastery.

The author visited there twice: the first time in the summer of 1916 during June and July, and then again in the summer of the following year for two weeks. At that time the Elder Anatole (Potapov) lived in the Optina Monastery itself; while Theodosius, the superior of the skete, and Fr. Nectarius lived in the skete about a half mile away from the monastery. A certain priest who was close to Optina characterized the spiritual personality of each of these Elders with a single word: "Theodosius, the sage; Anatole, the comforter; and the wondrous Nectarius." Fathers Anatole and Theodosius died in the first years of the Revolution, while Fr. Nectarius lived longer than all the others. He died in 1928, outside of the monastery when it had already been officially closed. My late mother and younger brother[1] would visit him several times a year, until the Elder's very death. And thus, through them, while already abroad, I had an opportunity to communicate with Fr. Nectarius, since during this period people were still permitted to correspond with relatives. But soon after Fr. Nectarius' death there ensued a long period of silence, and it was only during the war, in 1944, that the news arrived that my mother had died, having been tonsured a nun with the name of Nectaria, in memory of her Elder.

The ascetic labors of the Optina Monastery followed the ancient teaching of hesychasts; these practices were also known as "sobriety," or "mental activity." They originated when monasticism was first established during the time of Sts. Anthony the Great, Macarius of Egypt, John of the Ladder, and others. In later centuries the teachers of spiritual prayer were St. Gregory of Sinai

---

1. The future Bishop Nektary Kontzevitch (editor).

ELDER NECTARIUS OF OPTINA
spiritual father of the author.

An aquarelle by the author's sister Vera.

(†1346), a number of patriarchs of Constantinople, St. Gregory Palamas (†1360) the Archbishop of Thessalonica and other outstanding men of Byzantium, Bulgaria and Serbia; and later the Russian St. Nilus of Sora (†1508) and St. Paisius Velichkovsky (1722 - 1794).

The period when ascetic labors flourished among monastics also saw the spiritual rebirth of the entire Church, while the decline of such labors usually marked the decline of her spiritual life in general. Mental activity accompanied by eldership began in the early days of monasticism; but in the course of time they would start to flourish, reaching a significant development, and then would weaken or even sink into oblivion altogether, only to come to life again like the curve of a wave, now rising, now falling, and then rising again.

Thus, ascetic labor was forgotten also in Russia during the time of St. Paisius Velichkovsky in the 18th century. But this great Elder revived the spiritual practice of prayer and eldership, and they began to spread again throughout Russia's monasteries.

Although this meant the rebirth of ancient tradition in Russia itself, the majority of people considered these ascetic exercises, and the work of elders in particular, as incomprehensible innovations. Fr. Sergius Chetverikov says that the monastic activity of Russian elders has been insufficiently explored, and was not appreciated in pre-Revolutionary Russian society.[2] However, it has not been this society alone that has held only vague notions about elders; our new theological literature has not had time yet to delve into this problem. Professor Serebryansky writes: "The question of elders in ancient Russian monasteries has remained completely untouched in our scholarly literature. But judging by the Lives of the saints, eldership must have been *widespread*."[3]

As he became more closely involved with literature on elders and the Jesus Prayer, the author of the present work encountered certain opinions which were not the result of scholarly research, but were simply expressed *a priori*, and were often referred to as a case already established by scholars. Among these there is one about a break of ancient Russian sanctity with the Eastern tradition, which break allegedly occurred in the 14th and 15th centuries. At that time on Mt. Athos and in Byzantium people witnessed the flowering of contemplative endeavors which in the 14th century became known as "hesychasm." However, according to this *a priori* assertion, hesychasm could not reach us "for historical and geographical" reasons, and therefore the character of ancient Russian as-

---

2. Archpriest Sergius Chetverikov, "The History of Russian Eldership," in *Put* (Paris, September, 1925), p. 99.

3. S. Smirnov, *Ancient Russian Spiritual Father-Confessors* (Moscow, 1913), p. 26.

ceticism had, from then on, developed independently and in a unique manner, forming "a special branch of Orthodox sanctity."

One more circumstance should be noted here — an almost generally negative or at best indifferent, attitude toward hesychasm. This was noted both during the last century and at the beginning of the present century.[4] It is only recently that an interest in hesychasm has begun to emerge. This could be explained by the fact that Russian theology, which began to develop during Peter I's reforms under the influence of Western humanism, had not yet found its own direction. Western countries, on the other hand, from the very beginning of the so-called hesychast controversy of the 14th century, assumed negative attitudes towards this teaching. Moreover, during the last century, as a reaction following the reign of Alexander I and the preoccupation of certain people with Western mysticism, any kind of mysticism, even Orthodox mysticism, was approached with fear. As Professor Archpriest Georges Florovsky says: "Out of fear of mystical confusion and loss of balance people began to turn aside from the exhortations of both Macarius of Egypt and Isaac the Syrian, and the practice of mental prayer was abolished and ridiculed as a contagion and a pest."[5] Speaking of Peter's reign and pointing to the fact that "even theology was fashioned after the Western model" the professor notes the existence of a break in Church consciousness, "a break between theological scholarship and the actual experience of the Church."[6] This situation has continued up to our days. This leaning towards the West began a long time ago and progressed gradually. The

---

4. Let us, for example, consider the academic course in Patrology offered by Archbishop Philaret Gumilevsky (1805-1866): "Historical Teaching About the Church Fathers." The author prudently avoids analyzing the writings of the Holy Fathers on the subject of mental prayer. They are mentioned only in footnotes or are included in the general list. Even in a later period, in *Manual for Clergy* by S. V. Bulgakov (Kiev, 1913, p. 1622), hesychasts are spoken of as "being distinguished by the most unusual kind of dreaminess. They considered the navel as the center of spiritual energies and, consequently, the center of contemplation; and they thought that by lowering their chin towards the chest and gazing at the navel they would percieve the light of Paradise and rejoice in seeing celestial inhabitants. They considered this quiet concentration at one point as an indispensable condition for the perception of Uncreated Light." Due to the patronage of Emperor Andronicus Paleologus the Younger and the defense of St. Gregory Palamas, the hesychasts had victory over the Council of Constantinople in 1341, but "the outrageous opinion of the hesychasts concerning the reception of Uncreated Light was soon given over to oblivion." Bulgakov's book — this official handbook which was offered to all the clergy of such a large Orthodox land and which went through such severe spiritual censorship — demonstrates such complete ignorance of the question of hesychasm, naively repeating an old slander that had been levelled by its enemy Barlaam as far back as the 14th century.

5. Professor Archpriest Georges Florovsky, *Ways of Russian Theology* (Paris, 1937), p. 171.

6. *Ibid.*, p. 101.

moment of crisis was reached during the fall of Byzantium, when Moscow piety became doubtful of the purity of Greek piety.[7] Considering the break created "between theological scholarship and the actual experience of the Church," little interest in the study of Russian sanctity existed. It was historians who began exploring material on the Lives of saints. Thus, Professor Kliuchevsky in his famous work, *Ancient Russian Lives of Saints As a Source of History* (1871), has done a great deal of research on the Lives [of saints] exclusively for historical purposes. He explored over 150 documents on the Lives, seeking to extract from them historical data, but the results did not satisfy him. His task was continued, although primarily with regard to the saints of the North, by Yakhontov, who arrived at even less satisfactory results. From that time on scholars lost all interest in the Lives, until Professor Kadlubovsky, at the beginning of the 20th century once again returned to them, studying them as literary documents. Exploring the moral and religious views of the epoch, he would encounter expressions such as "inner work" or "spiritual activity" and the like, but paying tribute to his own time he was not interested in coming to terms with the essence of hesychasm and did not suspect that he was dealing with a specific terminology that had an entire school behind it.

In 1898, in Kiev, K. Radchenko's book *Religious and Literary Movements in Bulgaria Before the Turkish Invasion* was published. The work was entirely in the spirit of the time. Radchenko accused hesychasts of "pantheism" on the grounds that in the contemplation of God a man could somehow lose hold of his individual existence and fall into heresy. Besides, he stated, by shifting emphasis to the inward life, hesychasts were weakening Church authority. He decisively placed himself on the side of "Western rationalistic scholasticism" and

---

7. "And thus it happens," says Professor Archpriest Georges Florovsky, "that theological discourse takes place only in the West. Theology is in essence a problem to be worked out by catholicity, but it was tackled only in schism. This is a basic paradox in the history of Christian culture. The West engages in theological discourse, while the East keeps silent, or, what is even worse, unthinkingly and belatedly repeats the pattern of alien discourse" (*ibid.*, p. 515). Pointing to the root of the existing situation, Professor Archpriest Georges Florovsky says: "The crisis of Russian Byzantinism experienced in the 16th century marks also the falling away of Russian thought from the patristic tradition in theology; patristic style and method were lost. It is not enough to know patristic texts and to know how to choose the needed references and proofs. One should understand patristic theology from within. Intuition is probably more important than erudition: it alone can resurrect and revive the ancient texts and turn them into a 'witness'" (p. 506). "The reestablishment of patristic style is the first and basic postulate of the rebirth of Russian theology. It is not a matter of some kind of 'restoration' or simple repetition; nor of a return 'to the Fathers'; whatever comes, it must always be forward and not backwards. It is a matter of loyalty to the patristic spirit, not just to the letter; it is a matter of taking fire from the patristic flame, rather than 'herborizing' the ancient texts [collecting them as one collects plants] " (p. 506).

against "extravagant theosophic mysticism," etc. Somewhat later however, in the same year, the first part (600 pages) of a large five-volume work by P. Syrkou *A History of the Correction of Books in Bulgaria in the 14th Century* was published. This work was the result of profound scholarly research of the issue. In writing about the life and teaching of St. Gregory of Sinai, he revealed the true significance of hesychasm as the highest manifestation of the spiritual life of the Church. In his work, P. Syrkou evaluated Radchenko's book in the following words: "Given the position that some medieval mystics, hesychasts in particular, were depressed by the deadly dogmas of Christianity, Radchenko tried everywhere to seek out points of contact between hesychast and heretical teaching, and as a result he reached a false conclusion which was, moreover, not quite clearly expressed. This was the main purpose of Radchenko's book. All the remaining sections of the book were very weak."[8] It was also Radchenko who came up with the opinion, already mentioned above, that hesychasm of the 14th century could not possibly have reached Russia for "historical and geographical" reasons. This hypothesis has survived until now; hence, only its acceptance could have enabled Professor Fedotov to surmise the existence of a unique Russian sanctity — although what it is that constitutes this uniqueness has so far remained unclarified. He says: "They usually link our eldership or our fools-for-Christ with the *Philokalia*, casting bridges across a millenium and bypassing a completely unknown, or seemingly known sanctity of ancient Russia. Strange as it may be, the task of exploring Russian sanctity as a unique tradition of spiritual life has never been undertaken." In his last book, published in 1948 in New York in English, *A Treasury of Russian Spirituality*, Professor Fedotov writes as follows:

"In the middle of the 19th century the evangelical and humanitarian tendencies which largely dominated Russian secular literature tempted the ascetic spirituality of the Church. The slavophiles, a liberal national party in the Church, tried to create (or, rather, to resuscitate) a spirituality based on social ethic. But the breach between the ascetic-mystical and the evangelical elements within the Church widened, and each tendency found political expression in the period immediately preceding the Revolution. The evangelicals[9] stood for ecclesiastical reforms and allied themselves with the liberal political groups of the nation; the mystics supported the absolutism of the Tsar as a remnant of Byzantine tradition. The reformers and liberals did not succeed in developing a type of spirituality of their own deep enough to counterbalance the reactionary, or 'black'

---

8. P. Syrkou, *A History of the Correction of Books in Bulgaria in the 14th Century*, first edition, no. 1 (St. Petersburg, 1898), p. 6.

9. This term probably refers to the "Living Church."

influence of monasticism, and this dualism played a fatal part in the disintegration of the moral forces of pre-Revolutionary Russian society."[10]

Thus, both mysticism and sanctity, as viewed by Professor Fedotov, are reduced to phenomena of an already purely subjective nature, fully determined by the spirit of the epoch.

The negative attitude toward hesychasm, however, is being gradually replaced by the reestablishment of its true meaning not only in Orthodoxy but also among certain Western scholars. In 1930, in the Paris edition *Byzantine Art Among the Slavs* there appeared an article by a professor of Belgrade University, Milos Vasich, in which he explored the influence of hesychasm upon Serbian medieval art. He wrote that to perform this task he had, first of all, to use a strictly archeological method and, secondly, to recognize hesychasm as "a teaching of the official Church," repudiating "the still existing preconceived notion that maintained that hesychasm was nothing more than a sectarian teaching. . . ." "For a long time there existed an incorrect notion about hesychasm, but lately excellent apologists have been found (here Vasich means Western scholars) who have brought to attention the existence of this movement and presented it as it really was."

Thus, for instance, Helzer considers the struggle which arose over hesychasm to be "one of the most amazing phenomena of all times and one of the most interesting in the history of civilization, despite the generally accepted tale which is being taught in (Western) universities and seminaries under the name of "Church History," and which has never ceased pouring cheap mockery over hesychasm and thus only proving its complete misunderstanding of the most serious problem in the history of ideas." Professor Vasich further presents arguments offered by Hall, who "unhesitatingly regards the controversy over hesychasm, which has acquired such a bad reputation in the West, as the most significant moment in the history of the Greek Church. It was then for the first time that the Church became aware that she had treasured within herself this monastic enthusiasm which drew its strength from her bosom. It was clear that all dogmatic conclusions and arguments, hitherto apparently forgotten, had once again arisen in the society of that period. Learned theologians of the two camps were locked in this struggle, their dialectics bearing witness to the onset of a new rebirth of philosophy."

In 1936 Professor Ignatius Smolitch's book *The Life and Teaching of the Elders* (*Leben und Lehre der Startzen*, Vienna) came out in German. This book

---

10. G. P. Fedotov, *A Treasury of Russian Spirituality* [in English] (New York, 1948), pp. 15-16.

has also failed to contribute anything new towards shedding light on the problem of the nature of ancient Russian sanctity. Dr. Smolitch, like the others, supported the notion of the unique nature of Russian sanctity when he said that "experiences of a contemplative nature do not form a part of the essence of Russian ascetic practice except among a few Russian saints, only a few of whom could be called mystics." The virtue of his book, however, lies in the fact that the author's comprehensive examination and systematization of Orthodox mystical theology presents a clear idea about it and its correct characteristics.

Finally, hesychasm has found its complete and finite justification in the dissertation of Professor Archimandrite Cyprian (Kern) in *The Anthropology of St. Gregory Palamas*, published in 1950 in Paris. The author defends hesychasm with all the power of his scholarly erudition and offers a comprehensive investigation of the material relating to the problem in one way or another.

My first-hand acquaintance with the literature dealing with our topic shows that the nature of ancient Russian sanctity, eldership and its meaning still remains unclarified. I proceeded in the present study to present still more material on the subject, with the hope of achieving greater clarification. The historical part was organized as follows: as many Lives of Saints were explored as was possible (including Lives of monk-saints). The data obtained was organized chronologically, which helped to establish the character of the periods and the link of ancient Russian asceticism with that of the East.

This work is a further development of the candidate's thesis (1948) written under the guidance of a professor of the Theological Institute in Paris, A. V. Kartashev, to whom I am profoundly grateful for his lively interest in the subject and his serious criticism.

ST. ANTHONY THE GREAT
searching for and finding St. Paul of Thebes.

*A fresco by Archimandrite Cyprian (Pyzhov) from the refectory
of Holy Trinity Monastery, Jordanville, New York.*

PART I
(Introductory)

A BRIEF SURVEY OF ASCETICISM

(The Essence of "Inward Activity")

Banished from the Joys of Paradise, Adam sat outside and wept, and beating his hands upon his face he said: I am fallen, in Thy compassion have mercy on me.

When Adam saw the Angel drive him out and shut the door of the divine garden, he groaned aloud and said: I am fallen, in Thy compassion have mercy on me.

O Paradise, share in the sorrow of thy master who is brought to poverty, and with the sound of thy leaves pray to the Creator that He may not keep thy gate closed forever. I am fallen, in Thy compassion have mercy on me.

(Ikos for the Forgiveness Sunday Matins)

ST. SERAPHIM OF SAROV WITH N. A. MOTOVILOV

An illustration from the book St. Seraphim of Sarov *by A. P. Timofievich, published by New Diveyevo Convent, Spring Valley, New York.*

INTRODUCTION

ATRISTIC THEOLOGY is comprised of the works of the Church Fathers, as well as the service books of the Church. The wonderful harmony of these chants of the most exalted and pure poetry flows with ease, penetrating to the very depths of the soul. During the Matins of the Sunday before Lent, vivid and inimitable images speak of the state of the fallen Adam, expelled from Paradise and weeping over his "degradation": "I who was once king of all God's creatures upon earth have now become a prisoner. . . ." "I . . . must now, as one condemned to die, wrap myself miserably in skins of mortality." We all, the children of Adam, are prisoners of sin. The purpose of the way of asceticism is to cast off "the skins of mortality" and to become clothed in the grace of the Holy Spirit — the garment of the New Adam — which is Christ.

Before his Fall, Adam was inwardly collected by the divine grace inherent in him and he was creatively aspiring to reach God through perfect love for Him and conformance to His divine will. He was wholly immersed in contemplation of God and in communion with God. All manifestations of the triune nature of man (*i.e.*, the spirit, the soul and the body) harmoniously unified in him, hierarchically submitted to the highest principle within man — to his spirit. The spirit ruled over all aspects of human nature, directing them towards the single highest purpose. The first man was wholly filled with the grace of the Holy Spirit and emanated light, like St. Seraphim during his conversation with Motovilov.[1] The elements of the world were unable to harm man and he was immortal. Sin, this sting of death, introduced the poison of disintegration and corruption into the nature of man. Divine grace, which had until then protected and integrated him, now abandoned him. All the energies of his soul were now in the state of confusion and contradiction. The flesh rebelled against the spirit — the slave against his master. Thus, the order of man's soul became distorted, and there appeared a confused human being, the man of sin. Passion is not something new, brought in from without, but a redirection of former qualities and abilities from what is proper to what is wrong. Thus, the highest manifestation of the spirit, its ability to aspire to the most holy, towards God, upon the loss of communion with the Divine, turned downwards and exchanged these aspirations for the love of oneself and all things lowly and created.

In this way, self-love, egoism and other passions replaced by themselves the love for God. Theocentrism gave way to egocentrism. Left to his own resources, fallen man was now unable to arise through his own natural strength and to free himself of contradictions, passions, sin and suffering, to leave this vicious circle of death and the feeling of being abandoned by God. He began feeling the need for supernatural assistance. Thousands of years went by before the Redeemer appeared. St. John of Kronstadt said: "Before He became flesh, the Lord allowed man to experience all the bitterness of sin, all his helplessness in eradicating it; and when everyone cried out for the Savior — He appeared, the wise and powerful Physician and Helper. When truth became scarce and people began to hunger and thirst for it, then came the Truth eternal."[2] St. John of Damascus said: "By His birth, by becoming flesh, as well as through His baptism, suffering and resurrection, He delivered human nature from the forefather's sin, from death and corruption; He became the source of resurrection and declared Himself the Way, the image and the example, so that we, following in His footsteps and through adoption by Him, might become what He is by His nature: the sons and heirs of God and His co-heirs."[3] Thus Christ became the only mighty *power* of people's salvation (Rom. 1:4, I Cor. 1:24), *the captain of their salvation* (Heb. 2:10), the only *way* to God (John 14:6). Life in Christ is achieved through

---

1. "The original state of Adam before the Fall is considered to have been particularly perfect. Adam was 'clothed in glory,' in 'divine radiance and brilliance,' and 'partook of the Divine Light' (St. Gregory Palamas). The Transfiguration on Mount Tabor showed to the Apostles both the future glory of the Kingdom of God and the state of the pre-Fall paradisaical bliss lost by Adam." Professor Archimandrite Cyprian (Kern), *Anthropology of St. Gregory Palamas* (Paris, 1950), p. 403.

2. Archpriest John Sergiev (St. John of Kronstadt), *My Life in Christ*, Book 1 (Moscow), p. 158.

3. S. Zarin, *Asceticism*, Vol. I, Book 2 (St. Petersburg, 1907), pp. 32-33.

the Holy Mysteries. "Through the Holy Mysteries, as if through little windows, the Sun of Truth penetrates this dark world, destroying the life of this world and restoring the pre-worldly life; the Light of the world overcomes the world, as indicated by the Savior: *I have overcome the world.*" We will quote Archbishop Nicholas Cabasilas of Thessalonica (†1371) from his theological work on the meaning of the Mysteries — *The Life in Christ.* He compares human life with the seed of a plant put into the soil: "Truly this world carries the new inner man created in the image of God; being conceived here and fully formed, he is born in the other, unaging world. . . ." "The life in Christ," he says, "is conceived and begins in the present life, but is accomplished in the future life, when our day comes. . . . But even after death one will not partake of good things in heaven, if he has not acquired the necessary energies and feelings while living on earth; he will be an unhappy and dead man in a happy and immortal world, the reason being that, although light will be shining there abundantly, one will need the eyes to perceive this light, and the sense of smell to perceive the fragrance pervading there. Only the Holy Mysteries may give birth to the organs of perception of spiritual life, which 'on that day' would enable man to enter into communion with Christ and His friends, and to learn from Him what He heard from the Father. However, one should come to Him being His friend and having ears. One will not be able to befriend anyone there, nor to open his ears and prepare the wedding garment, because the present life (on earth) is given for such preparations; and those who will be lacking all this before departing from this life, will have nothing in common with the future life."

In His Mysteries, the Lord "being the Nurturer, is at the same time the Nourishment; He gives the bread of life, being the bread Himself. He is the life of the living, the myrrh of those who breathe, and the garment of those who wish to be appropriately attired. It is only with Him that we can walk, because He is the Way, the Rest on the Way and its Destination."[4] But one should not restrict oneself to a mechanical assimilation of the Mysteries. It is essential that one desire them and make an effort, of which Christ spoke: *The Kingdom of Heaven suffereth violence, and the violent take it by force* (Matt. 11:12). Salvation requires cooperation between grace and the free will of man, who should choose the way of ascetic struggles.

Let us examine the meaning of the concept of "asceticism." According to the research done by Professor Zarin, ἀσκόί, as used by Homer, denoted wineskin. Philologists assume that ἀσκέω meant treatment of skin. Later "ascesis"

---

4. Nicholas Cabasilas, *La Vie en Jesus Christ (The Life in Jesus Christ)* (Prieure d' Amay sur Meuse, 1932), 236 pp.

meant gymnastic exercises, and still later in philosophy it meant achieving virtue by means of exercises. The Apostle Paul (I Cor. 9:24-27) used this concept in two contemporary meanings: training as exercise to win in competitive games, and spiritual exercise designed to combat vice and develop virtue. In patristic writings the term "ascesis" was commonly used in the meaning of: fasting, praying, solitude, vigil and other endeavors and deprivations.

Christian religions vary in their attitude towards asceticism. The Roman Catholic Church regards it as a discipline compulsory for monastics, and something "over and above the norm" for lay people. Protestant Churches simply reject asceticism. Orthodox teaching, however, is that asceticism, although to various extents and to various forms, is obligatory for all Christians without exception, according to the words of the Savior, Who requires that His followers make an effort.[5]

---

5. Zarin, *Asceticism,* Vol. I, Book 2, pp. 1-15.

Chapter One

THE ORDER OF
SPIRITUAL ASCENT

THE WAY TO GOD leads through knowledge of oneself. "No one can know God without knowing himself," repeats St. Athanasius the Great after St. Anthony the Great. The knowledge of oneself is the greatest of sciences, since no one who has not mastered it will ever know God. An ascetic needs to have the knowledge of spiritual and psychological laws and a deep insight into his own soul. Usually, however, people suffer from blindness and self-delusion and are unable to see their fallen state. Therefore, becoming aware of one's own true state and of evil within oneself is the first step towards knowledge of oneself. On this path towards impassibility, however, an ascetic is faced with a very difficult and long warfare against passions, and with an acquisition of virtues. This is a gradual process and must be accomplished in the proper order. St. Isaac the Syrian (7th century) says: "Every virtue is the mother of the one following it. If one should leave the mother who is giving birth to other virtues, and aspire to seek out the daughters before attaining their mother, these virtues turn into vipers within one's soul. If one dismisses them, one will soon die."[1] Thus, spiritual perfection is attained gradually and in a definite order, like building a house. On its foundation of faith one should place the stones of obedience, endurance, abstinence, and on these — the stones of compassion, renunciation of one's own will, etc., the cornerstones being patience and courage, which give the house its

---

1. St. Isaac the Syrian, *Works* (Sergiev Posad, 1893), p. 363.

firm stability. Like a cement holding everything together, so is humility, without which not a single good deed is an act of virtue, nor is it possible to be saved.[2] *"Humility* is Christ's spiritual doctrine, noetically introduced into the inner chamber of the soul by those who are accounted worthy of it. It cannot be defined by perceptible words."[3] The Lord says of Himself: *For I am meek and lowly in heart* (Matt. 11:29). "Learn not from an angel, nor from man, nor from a book, but from Me, that is, from My indwelling, from My illumination and action in you."[4] The Holy Mother of God speaks of her humility: *For He hath regarded the low estate of His handmaiden* (Luke 1:48). According to St. John of the Ladder there are three degrees of humility. The first belongs to those who have achieved dispassion, the second to those who are manly-minded, and the third — the lower — is indispensable to all Christians.[5] "Without humility, no one will enter the bridal chamber."[6] "Humility is a heavenly siphon from which the abyss of sins can raise the soul to heaven."[7] For "humility even without good deeds renders many sins pardonable, because without humility all our good deeds, all the various virtues and actions, are futile."[8] One can attain humility only through experience. When practicing mental prayer and spiritual struggles, man becomes convinced that despite all his efforts he is helpless. It is then that he actually becomes aware of God's help and afraid to lose it through his self-reliance; therefore he ascribes nothing to himself, but everything to God alone, referring to his endeavors as follows: "I have done only what I was commanded to do, worthless slave that I am."[9] "If anyone says: 'I am rich, I am satisfied with what I have acquired, and have no need for more' — he is not a Christian, but a vessel of *prelest* (delusion) and of Satan. One cannot ever have enough happiness in God; and to what extent he tastes and partakes of it, to that extent he thirsts for more. Such people are full of fervor and irrepressible love for God. The more they strive to accomplish and acquire in their fervor, the more they consider themselves as being poor and having acquired nothing. They think: I am unworthy for this sun to shine upon me. This is the true mark of Christianity — this is humility."[10] Such is the self-awareness of an Orthodox ascetic, and herein

---

2. According to Abba Dorotheos, in Zarin, *Asceticism*, p. 12.
3. St. John Climacus, *The Ladder* (Holy Trinity-St. Sergius Lavra, 1898), Step 25, verse 41.
4. *Ibid.*, verse 3.
5. *Ibid.*, verse 49.
6. *Ibid.*, verse 52.
7. *Ibid.*, verse 68.
8. St. Isaac the Syrian, *Works*, Homily 46, p. 202.
9. *Cf.* Luke 17:10 *(editor)*.
10. St. Macarius of Egypt, *Homilies* (Holy Trinity-St. Sergius Lavra, 1904), p. 129.

lies the difference between the Orthodox and the Roman Catholic points of view. The concept of "over and above the norm" merits are inadmissible in Eastern understanding. As early as the 5th century, St. Hesychius of Jerusalem taught: "The Heavenly Kingdom is not a reward for good deeds, but rather the gift of grace of the Master, prepared for His faithful slaves. A slave does not demand freedom as a reward; but having received it he expresses his gratitude as a debtor, and not having received it, he waits for it as for alms."[11] A true ascetic does not demonstrate his humility; he does not show off or talk humility. "The most dangerous kind of pride is to think of oneself as a humble person; when a man takes his pride for humility, it cannot be easily eradicated."[12]

11. Archimandrite Cyprian, *Anthropology of St. Gregory Palamas*, p. 399.
12. Bishop Ignatius Brianchaninov, *Works*, Vol. I (St. Petersburg, 1865), pp. 619-620.

ANCIENT DESERT MONASTERIES
where ascetic struggle has been practiced for fifteen centuries.

Above: the Monastery of St. Macarius the Great in
Scetis of the Egyptian Thebaid, as it looks today.
Below: the Monastery of St. Sabbas the Sanctified in
Palestine, near Bethlehem. *An aquarelle painted in 1839.*

Chapter Two

THE STRUGGLE WITH PASSIONS

PASSIONS, LIKE VIRTUES, are also interconnected, just as "links of a single chain" (St. Isaac of Nitria), one being an offshoot of another. There are eight of them; in the order of birth they are as follows: 1) gluttony, 2) lust, 3) avarice, 4) anger, 5) despondency, 6) despair, 7) vainglory, and 8) pride.

The main concern of patristic asceticism is not with external manifestations of sin, nor individual instances of sin, but rather with their cause, *i.e.*, the vices and passions rooted in the soul, or diseases of the soul and hidden inner states of sin. Using contemporary terms and concepts, Professor Zarin expounds the teaching of the Holy Fathers about the psychology of passion and the struggle with it. Here is a brief resume of this exposition.

A thought is the initial moment in the emergence of a passion; it is a moment of hesitation and an essential central element of this psychological state.[1] The essence of asceticism amounts to the struggle with thoughts. The Holy Fathers, ascetics, discern as many as [six or] seven moments in the development and growth of passions.

1. PROVOCATION (SUGGESTION)

The first impetus to the emergence of the psychological phenomenon which may end as passion is known as a "provocation" or "suggestion" (*prilog*).

---

1. There are three main moments: 1) the appearance of a concept, 2) the adding to it of the feeling, and 3) the adding to it of the will. (Mind, feeling, will: a concept, in conjunction with feeling and with the addition of the will.)

It is a conception of an object or an action corresponding to one of the stained inclinations within a person. Under the influence of external impressions, or in connection with the psychological working of the memory or imagination according to the laws of association, this provocation enters the sphere of man's consciousness. This first moment takes place independently of man's free will, against his wish, without his participation, in accordance with the laws of psychological inevitability — "spontaneity" — and is, therefore, considered "innocent" or dispassionate. It does not incriminate man in sin if it is not caused by his "wandering" thoughts, if it is not invited consciously and voluntarily, and if a person is not negligent about it. This is the touchstone for testing our will, to see whether it will be inclined towards virtue or vice. It is in this choice that the free will of man manifests itself.[2]

2. CONJUNCTION

Provocation evokes the response of the *feeling*, which reacts to the impression or image intruding upon the consciousness by either "love" or "hate" (sympathy or antipathy). This is the most important moment, for it decides the fate of the provoking thought: will it stay, or will it flee? It is only the emergence of this thought in the consciousness that occurs regardless of the will of man. If it is not immediately rejected and lingers on, this means that in the nature of a given person it finds compatable ground, which is expressed in his sympathetic reaction to the provocation. Sympathetic inclination attracts *attention*, allowing the suggested thought to grow and turn into an image of fantasy pervading the entire sphere of consciousness and ousting all other impressions and thoughts. Attention lingers at the thought because man *delights* in it. This second moment is called *conversation* or *conjunction* (*sochetanie*). St. Ephraim the Syrian defines it as a "free acceptance of the thought, its entertainment, as it were, and a conversation with it accompanied by delight." In the contemporary language of psychology this means that the second moment in the development of the thought lies in the following: man's attention is directed exclusively to the newly arisen impression or notion, which serves as an impetus or cause for the development of a whole series of associated notions. These notions give man the feeling of pleasure while anticipating the enjoyment of the object of the impression or notion obtained. In order to cut off the sequence of notions, to remove it from his consciousness, and to terminate the feeling of delight, man

---

2. There are two causes for the occurrence of "provocation": natural causes and evil spirits.

needs to *distract* his attention by the effort of his will. He must actively and firmly resolve to rebut the images of sin assailing him and not return to them again.

3. JOINING

Otherwise, with the absence of willful rejection of the intruding images, the third moment is induced, when the will itself becomes increasingly attracted to the thought, and as a result man becomes *inclined* to act upon what the thought tells him and to get the satisfaction of partaking of it. At this time the equilibrium of his spiritual life is totally destroyed, the soul wholly surrenders itself to the thought and *strives* to realize it with the purpose of experiencing an even more intense delight. Thus, the third moment is characterized by the *inclination of will* towards the object of the thought, by its agreement and resolve to realize pleasurable fantasies. Consequently, in the third moment the whole will surrenders to the thought and now acts according to its directives in order to realize its fantastic plans. This moment, called *joining* (*slozhenie*), is the cooperation of the will, which is a declaration of agreement with the passion whispered by the thought (St. Ephraim the Syrian), or *consent* of the soul to what has been presented to it by the thought, accompanied by delight (St. John of the Ladder). This state is already "approaching the act of sin and is akin to it" (St. Ephraim the Syrian). There comes the willful *resolve* to attain the realization of the object of the passionate thought by all means available to man. In principle, the decision has already been made to satisfy the passion. Sin has already been committed in intention. It now remains to satisfy the sinful desire, turning it into a concrete act.

4. STRUGGLE

Sometimes, however, before man's final decision to proceed to this last moment, or even after such a decision, he experiences a struggle between the sinful desire and the opposite inclination of his nature.

5. HABIT

However, the last psychological moment of an unstable vacillation of the will between opposing inclinations takes place only when the *habit* has not yet been formed within the soul, namely, the "bad habit" of responding to the evil thought. It takes place when a sinful inclination has not yet deeply penetrated man's nature and become a constant feature of his character, a familiar element of his disposition, when his mind is constantly preoccupied with the object of the passionate urge, when the passion itself has not yet been completely formed.

6. CAPTIVITY

When in the power of passion, man gladly and violently rushes to satisfy this passion, either without any struggle at all, or almost without a struggle. He is losing the dominant, guiding and controlling power of his volitional faculty over individual inclinations and demands of volitional nature. It is no longer the will that rules over sinful inclinations, but the latter rule over the will, forcibly and wholly enticing the soul, compelling its entire rational and active energy to concentrate on the object of passion. This state is called *captivity* (*plenenie*). This is the moment of the complete development of a passion, of the fully established state of the soul, which now manifests all of its energy to the utmost.[3]

"The best and the most successful struggle takes place when the thought is cut off by means of an unceasing prayer at the very start. For, as the Fathers have said, whoever opposes the *initial thought*, *i.e.*, the provocation, will stop its subsequent disposition at once. A wise ascetic destroys the mother of wicked fiends, *i.e.*, the cunning provocation (first thoughts). At the time of prayer, above all else, one's intellect should be rendered deaf and mute (St. Nilus of Sinai), and one's heart emptied of any thoughts, even a seemingly good thought (St. Hesychius of Jerusalem). Experience has shown that the admission of a dispassionate thought, *i.e.*, a distraction, is followed by an impassioned (wicked) one, and that the entry of the first opens the door to the latter."[4]

This inner struggle is vividly portrayed to us by St. Hesychius of Jerusalem (5th century), a disciple of St. Gregory the Theologian:

No. 145. Our mind, being something of light appearance and innocent, easily gives itself over to daydreaming and is unrestrainedly subject to evil thoughts, if it does not have in itself such a concept which, like a monarch over the passions, holds it constantly under control and bridles it.

No. 168. A ship does not move without water; and there is no progress whatsoever in the guarding of the mind without sobriety with humility and prayer to Jesus Christ.

No. 169. Stones are used for the foundation of a house; but for this virtue (the guarding of the mind) both the foundation and the root are the holy

---

3. Zarin, *Asceticism*, Vol. I, Book 2, pp. 248-258.
4. *St. Nilus of Sora* (Moscow, 1869), p. 19.

and venerable name of our Lord Jesus Christ. Quickly and easily can a foolish captain wreck his ship during a storm, dismissing the sailors, throwing the sails and oars into the sea, and going to sleep himself; but much more quickly can the soul be drowned by the demons if, when the thoughts begin to emerge, it does not guard sobriety, and invoke the name of Jesus Christ.

No. 94. Sobriety and the Jesus Prayer mutually reinforce one another; for extreme watchfulness goes with the content of constant prayer, while prayer goes with extreme sobriety and watchfulness of intellect.

No. 88. Many of our thoughts come from demonic suggestions, and from these derive our evil outward actions. If with the help of Jesus we instantly quell the thought, we will avoid its corresponding outward action. We will enrich ourselves with the sweetness of divine knowledge and so will find God, Who is everywhere. Holding the mirror of the intellect firmly towards God, we will be illumined constantly as pure glass is by the sun. Then finally the intellect, having reached the limit of its desires, will in Him cease from all other contemplation.[5]

5. St. Hesychius of Jerusalem, *Exhortations on Watchfulness and Prayer* (Moscow, 1890). [English translation in *The Philokalia* (G. E. H. Palmer, et al.), Vol. I.]

VISION OF THE HEAVENLY LADDER
St. John Climacus stands at the foot of the Ladder, guiding monks up its steps.
Icon of the Moscow School, 16th century.

Chapter Three

PRAYER

The virtue of prayer performs the mystery of our union with God; it is the tie of rational creatures with their Creator (St. Gregory Palamas) *and is the leader of the host of virtues. Not one of them is stable without prayer.* (St. Gregory of Nyssa)

1. THE JESUS PRAYER, ANCIENT AND UNCEASING

BESIDES ST. HESYCHIUS OF JERUSALEM (5th century), other ancient Church Fathers also dealt with the Jesus Prayer. This was also pointed out by Ivan V. Kireyevsky in his letter (1855) to Elder Macarius of Optina: "Because some Western theologians disclaim the ancientness of this prayer (the unceasing Prayer of Jesus), it would be a good idea to point out the references in patristic writings which relate to the Prayer either directly or by allusion." With regard to the Jesus Prayer, Kireyevsky found advice given by St. Barsanuphius the Great (6th century) in his Answer no. 39. In no. 126 it is given in full: "Unceasing calling upon the name of God cures one not only of passions, but also of actions; and as a medicine affects a sick man without his comprehension, similarly the invocation of the name of God destroys passions in a manner beyond our comprehension." No. 424: "The name of Jesus should be invoked not only at the time of temptations, because unceasing calling of God's name is actually prayer." No. 425: "Invocation of God's name stops evil thoughts arising during psalmody, or prayer, or reading. (Consequently the Jesus Prayer should not cease during the recitation of other prayers. Fr. Seraphim made the same point when speaking to Fr. Archimandrite.)"[1] No. 429: "Not only in invoking God with the lips, but also in remembering Him in the heart, does prayer occur, for God is the knower of hearts and listens to the heart."[2]

The action of God's Name in prayer is explained by the Orthodox teaching on the Names of God:

"1. God's Name is holy, venerable and desirable, because it denotes in words the most aspired to and the holiest of beings — God, the Fount of all good things. This Name is Divine, because it has been revealed to us by God, it speaks to us of God, uplifts our intellect to God, etc. In a prayer (particularly in the Jesus Prayer) the Name of God and God Himself are perceived by us inseparably, as if identifying one another; they cannot and should not be separated or opposed to one another, although this is so only in prayer and only in our hearts. However, in theology as well as in actual fact, God's Name is only a name, not God Himself or His characteristics; it is a name of an object, not the object itself, and therefore it cannot be acknowledged or called either God (which would be absurd and blasphemous), or Divinity, because it is not the Energy of God.

"2. The Name of God, when uttered during prayer with faith, may even perform miracles, but not by itself, not as a consequence of some divine power forever contained in it or attached to it and acting mechanically, but because the Lord, seeing our faith (Matt. 9:2) and by virtue of His true promise, sends His grace and by it performs miracles."[3] (From the Holy Synod's Address of 1913 to monastics, in connection with the "Name-worshipping" heresy which arose in St. Panteleimon Monastery on Mt. Athos.)

2. THE STRUCTURE OF THE SOUL

In order to understand the most profound movement of prayer upon the soul, let us examine its structure. The soul of a man, this "object of his personal life" (Professor Zarin), is distinguished from the soul of an animal by its likeness to God: *Let us make man in Our image, after Our likeness* (Gen. 1:26), said God,

---

1. Fr. Seraphim — this is St. Seraphim of Sarov; Fr. Archimandrite — this is the Superior of the Optina Monastery, Archimandrite Moses who, while still a novice named Timothy, heard St. Seraphim's wonderful exhortation: "When standing in church one should pray with the Jesus Prayer to fully comprehend the church service." *Life of Archimandrite Moses* (Moscow, 1882), p. 12.
2. Chetverikov, *Optina Monastery* (Paris, 1926), pp. 134-135.
3. S. V. Troitsky, *On the Name of God* (St. Petersburg, 1914), p. 10.

and He *breathed* into the man *the breath of life* (Gen. 2:7), the spirit, *pneuma* — the God-like principle in the soul of man. The basic manifestations of the spirit are consciousness and freedom. The life of the soul, all its manifestations, states and feelings occur in the heart. The heart is a direct and unifying organ of life. Man's entire individual life is concentrated in his heart. The heart and the spirit are closely bound in an uninterrupted mutual activity. Activity of the spirit takes place predominantly in the heart, and man's conscience is the result of its action (Rom. 2:15). The source of the highest religious and moral life lies in the spirit, and it is through the spirit that man's living bond with God is established, since the spirit is the organ of *God's witness* (Rom. 8:16). The Spirit of God penetrates man's heart through his spirit and acts in it. Thus, the heart is a vessel of faith and religious consciousness, and conversely, when they are absent the heart may become the source of unbelief and all kinds of sinful states: *Out of the heart proceed evil thoughts, murders, adulteries, fornications, thefts, false witness, blasphemies* (Matt. 15:19). The organ of the spirit is the intellect, and they are closely bound. Its activity manifests itself in apprehension of abstract theoretical principles, as well as moral and practical principles. Due to the effect of the spirit upon it, the intellect is capable of apprehending that which is deposited in the soul, and religious and moral principles. But, as we said before, the heart is the focal point of all man's activities, of his entire life, including also his spirit. Thus, it also comprises and controls the activity of the intellect.

3. THE DESCENT OF THE MIND INTO THE HEART

The heart, or the ability to feel, this "center of life" both physical and spiritual, this "root of the human being," this "focal point of all his spiritual and animal-bodily forces" "lies deeper" than the active capabilities of the soul, namely the mind and the will, constituting as it were their foundation. And since the mind is the contemplative force, while the "heart" embraces the most profound individual experiences, their natural relation must be expressed in terms of constant and unremitting control of the "mind" over the "heart."[4] The intellect

---

4. "The concept of the heart occupies the central position in mysticism," says Professor Vysheslavtsev. "The heart means a certain depth, a hidden center of a person, wherein lies his value, his eternity. It is only in the mysterious depths of the heart that an encounter with God is possible. One can perceive Christ only with his heart: *Christ may dwell in your heart by faith* (Eph. 3:17). The heart is the center of love, while love is an expression of the deepest essence of a person. . . . It is the center not only of the conscious, but of the unconscious (subconscious) as well; not only of the soul, but also of the spirit; not only of what is comprehensible, but also of what is incomprehensible. The heart is God-like freedom. . . .

must communicate the proper direction to the heart, guarding it from sinful thoughts and leading it to virtuous thoughts. In view of the fact that thoughts emerge in the heart, man's attention should be kept close to or within the heart; this may be defined as "watchfulness of the mind over thoughts." In asceticism, this is termed as "abiding in the heart." The mind, abiding in the heart and watching over thoughts, must lock the attention in the words of the prayer. The forms of prayer are as follows. At first the prayer should be practiced only vocally. Later, as the mind begins to heed the movement of the tongue, the prayer becomes mental. Finally, there may ensue the "descent of the mind into the heart," as the Fathers say. Returning into the heart, the mind elicits the warmth of divine love within it, and thus inspires it to call upon the name of Jesus Christ freely and with inexpressible sweetness, to pray to God unceasingly and with tenderness: *I sleep but my heart waketh* (Song of Solomon 5:2).[5]

This "descent of the mind into the heart," or their union, is interpreted by Bishop Ignatius Brianchaninov in the following way: "The heart or the place of the heart, the rational power or the spirit of man, has its seat in the upper part of the heart under the left nipple of the breast, as the mind has its seat in the brain. At the time of prayer the spirit should join the mind; the mind prays in words uttered only mentally, or vocally as well, while prayer of the spirit is expressed by a feeling of tenderness, or by tears. This union is the gift of divine grace; for the beginner, however, it should suffice if his spirit sympathizes and cooperates with the mind. Provided the mind keeps its attention fixed on the prayer, the spirit will certainly experience the feeling of contrition."[6]

Man is like God and he is a little god (*ye are gods*) in his faculty of *freedom*, with which he was initially endowed 'in essence,' in his ability to say 'yes' or 'no,' 'may it be' or 'may it not be,' in the ability to act positively or negatively. This power is the very essence, the mysterious and wondrous essence of every 'I,' of every spirit. . . . At the basis of every act lies freedom (hence the choice between good and evil). The heart is the light of the Logos, the light of self-consciousness in the loftiest mystical sense of the word. . . . Speaking in Plato's language, one may say that the soul itself is the *contemplation of ideas*, and this constitutes its highest essence. It is 'logical' and contemplative. . . . It is not at all only the intellect which comprehends, contemplates and perceives: *comprehension* is broader than thinking, than intellectual knowledge. The heart, too, is the organ of comprehension; it comprehends many things inaccessible even to the intellect; it comprehends sanctity, beauty, value. Besides an intellectual comprehension, there is also an emotional comprehension. We arrive at the initial Biblical meaning of the heart: the heart is the organ of comprehension if we consider the latter in all its breadth and extending beyond the limits of scientific knowledge. In order to comprehend much of what is inaccessible to an isolated intellect, one needs to 'stand with his mind in the heart,' because, in the last analysis, the mind is rooted and centered in the heart, since a person has only one hidden center." B. Vysheslavtsev, *The Heart in Christian and Hindu Mysticism* (Paris, 1929), pp. 5, 9, 65, 67, 69, 70, 75.

5. Zarin, *Asceticism*, Vol. I, Book 2, pp. 372-380, 392-394, 576-586.
6. Bishop Ignatius Brianchaninov, *Works*, Vol. I, p. 157.

As mentioned above, the attention must abide in the upper part of the heart. The importance and significance of this instruction becomes evident in the following words of Elder Paisius Velichkovsky: "From the very beginning, one should train one's mind to stay, at the hour of prayer, in the upper part of the heart, looking into its depths and not at the side or at the bottom end. This point is important, because when the mind stays praying in the upper region of the heart, it is like a king sitting above his subjects. It can freely observe sinful thoughts splashing below and destroy them like the second babes of Babylon against the rock of Christ's Name. Also, being significantly removed from the loins, it can easily avert the burning desire of the flesh which has become inherent in our nature since Adam's fall into sin."[7]

By way of the continuous induction of God's Name into the soul, Christ's image penetrates man's subconsciousness and then flowers in his consciousness. The soul undergoes the process of transfiguration, beginning with its hidden depth and ending in its own "deification," as expressed in the Apostle's words: *Yet not I, but Christ liveth in me.* This, then, is the purpose and meaning of the Jesus Prayer.[8]

Prayer and watchfulness are inseparably bound. According to Professor Zarin's definition: "Watchfulness is the 'attention' of the mind towards what takes place in the 'heart' (*i.e.*, in the inner life), attention which is acquired through care, effort and experience, and accompanied by 'vigilance,' *i.e.*, continuous 'guarding' of the heart against sinful movements with the purpose of purifying it."

This ascetic endeavor is also known under various other names, giving it other shades of meaning: "*podvig* and labor of the mind" (St. Macarius the Great, St. John Cassian), "focusing oneself in one place" (St. Isaac the Syrian, St. Basil the Great) or else "self-concentration," "concentration within" (Bishop Theophan the Recluse), "inward activity" (Ancient Patericon, Bishop Theophan the Recluse), "activity of the heart" (Bishop Theophan the Recluse), "hidden activity," "spiritual activity" (St. Hesychius).[9]

---

7. *Anthology on the Jesus Prayer* (Valaam Monastery edition, 1936), p. 214; also, *The Life and Writings of the Moldavian Elder Paisius Velichkovsky* (Moscow, 1847), p. 128.
8. *The Way of a Pilgrim* (Paris, 1933), p. 7.
9. Zarin, *Asceticism*, Vol. I, Book 2, p. 587.

ST. (BISHOP) IGNATIUS BRIANCHANINOV
A true teacher of spiritual life and a Holy Father for modern times
(see p. 206).

A daguerreotype made when he was an archimandrite.

Chapter Four

SPIRITUAL CONTEMPLATION

THE HOLY FATHERS say that lofty spiritual states are attained only through the "guarding of the mind." According to St. Hesychius: "The guarding of the intellect may appropriately be called 'light-producing,' 'lightning-producing,' 'light-giving' and 'fire-bearing,' for truly it surpasses endless virtues, bodily or otherwise. Because of this, and because of the glorious light to which it gives birth, one must honor this virtue with worthy names. Those who are seized by love for this virtue are enabled, from being worthless sinners, ignorant, profane, uncomprehending and unjust, to become just, responsive, pure, holy and wise through Jesus Christ. Not only this, but they are able to contemplate mystically and theologize; and when they have become contemplatives, they bathe in a sea of pure and infinite light, touching it ineffably and living and dwelling in it. They have tasted *that the Lord is good*."[1]

According to St. Macarius of Egypt, the fire of grace, set aflame in the hearts of Christians by the Holy Spirit, makes them glow like candles before the face of the Son of God.

"Divine fire, in accordance with the will of a person, either flares up into a large flame, or dies down without any reflection in hearts confused by passions. The immaterial and divine fire illumines and tries souls. This fire descended upon the Apostles in the shape of tongues. This fire shone upon St. Paul, spoke

---

1. St. Hesychius of Jerusalem, *Exhortations on Watchfulness and Prayer*, no. 171.

to him and illumined his mind, blinding his eyes at the same time because no flesh can bear the radiance of this light. Moses saw this light in the unconsumed bush. This light, in the form of a chariot of fire, raised Elias up from the earth. Angels and serving spirits partake of the light of this fire. . . . This fire banishes demons and eradicates sins. This light is the power of the resurrection, the truth of eternal life, the dawning of the souls of saints, the continuity of the heavenly power" (St. Macarius of Egypt).

This, then, is the "Divine Energies," "the rays of Divinity" of which St. Dionysius the Areopagite speaks, the creative powers which penetrate the universe and are apprehended outside the created world as the inaccessible light, the abode of the Holy Trinity. These Energies, bestowed upon Christians through the Holy Spirit, are no longer external phenomena, but grace and inner light, which transform man's nature, deifying it. "God is called the Light, not after His nature, but in accordance with His Energy," says St. Gregory Palamas.[2] God is the Light inasmuch as He is revealed, communicated and apprehended. If God is called the Light it is only by analogy with the material light. The Divine Light has not only an allegorical and abstract meaning: it is the fact of mystical experience. This divine experience is granted to every man according to his strength and to a greater or lesser extent, depending on the worth of the man experiencing it. Perception of Divinity enveloped in the radiance of Uncreated Light is the "mystery of the eighth day," and it belongs to the future age. However, those who are accounted worthy may see *the Kingdom of God come with power* (Mark 9:1) already in this life, as the three Apostles saw it on Mt. Tabor.[3]

In the writings of St. Simeon the New Theologian we find an inspired description of the most exalted states of divine contemplation. He says: "God does not appear in some kind of an outline or fixed image, but as a simple yet incomprehensible and inexpressible formation of light, without an image. More than this I am unable to say. He appears clearly, though, and is well recognizable. He is perceived, although *purely invisibly*; He speaks and hears invisibly. God talks naturally with those who are born by Him as *gods through grace*, as men talk with one another, face to face; He loves His sons as their Father and is loved by them to the utmost; they see Him as a wondrous vision and they hear His voice in fear, but neither can they speak of this experience properly, nor can they keep silent about it. . . . They cannot have enough of the truth they hear proclaimed, because they are no longer masters over themselves, but the organs of

---

2. Vladimir Lossky, *Essai sur la Theologie Mystique de l'Eglise d'Orient* (Paris, 1944), pp. 217-218.
3. *Ibid.*

the Holy Spirit abiding within them, Who affects them and is, in turn, affected by them. . . ."

St. Simeon addresses Divinity, saying: "Once, when Thou didst come and wash me, immersing me repeatedly in the waters, as it seemed, I saw lightning flashing around me and rays of light emanating from Thy countenance and blending with the waters; seeing myself washed in luminous, radiant waters I fell into ecstasy. . . . Some time went by, and then I saw another awesome mystery. I saw Thee ascend to heaven and take me up with Thee. However, I do not know whether Thou didst take me there in the body or without it; Thou alone knowest it, for Thou hast done it. After being there with Thee for some length of time, wondering at the greatness of glory (I do not know either whose glory it was, or what it meant), I fell into ecstasy from its infinite loftiness, and I trembled. But then Thou didst leave me again alone on the earth where I stood before. Having come to myself, I realized that I was weeping and wondering at my sorrowful impoverishment. A while later Thou didst deign to show me Thy countenance shining like the sun, without image and invisible, from on high through the open skies. . . .

"Again Thou didst appear, invisible, intangible, imperceptible . . . and Thou didst allow me to see Thy glory even more abundantly. All the while Thou wast growing larger and spreading Thy radiance more and more; and as the darkness disappeared Thou didst seem to come closer and closer, as we experience when observing sensory things. For, when the moon shines and the clouds swiftly drift by in the wind, it seems that the moon itself moves faster, although in reality it keeps its usual pace.

"Thus, O Lord, it seemed to me that Thou, being motionless, wast coming towards me; being unchangeable, wast growing larger; and having no image, didst assume an image. Sometimes a blind man who gradually grows accustomed to seeing and taking the whole image of another man, or the entire outline of a human body portrays him little by little within himself the way he is, when the likeness of a person's image is being outlined in the eyes and through them passes into the mind, being imprinted in his memory as on a tablet. So Thou too, having completely purified my mind, didst clearly appear to me in the Light of the Holy Spirit; and as my mind perceived Thee more clearly and perfectly, it seemed to me as if Thou wast stepping out of somewhere, brightly radiant, and allowing me to see the features of Thine imageless countenance. . . . When I asked Thee, saying, 'O my Lord, Who art Thou?' then, for the first time Thou didst grant me to hear Thy sweet voice, and Thou didst talk to me with such sweetness and meekness that I fell into ecstasy, trembling in amazement, thinking and speaking to myself: 'How glorious and resplendent this is!' Thou hast told me: 'I am God become man, out of My love for thee. I am speaking to thee through the Holy Spirit, Who speaks to thee together with me. This I have given thee only because of thy desire and thy faith, and I shall give thee even more than this. . . . ' "

Under the impress of this divine contemplation, St. Simeon exclaimed in rapture: "What else could be more resplendent and exalted than this?" And he heard an answer, that the apprehension of the future life is higher than this happiness. "Thy soul is extremely small," heard St. Simeon, "if thou art satisfied with this happiness, because in comparison with the future bliss it is like a drawing of the sky on paper that someone holds in his hands in comparison with the real skies; even much more does the future glory surpass the one thou hast witnessed now."[4]

"Palamas, too, knew of an illumination of the inner man by the inexpressible light, when this light guides him along the path leading to the eternal heights and he becomes the beholder of supernatural things. . . . " According to him, an ascetic, "detaching himself from the material world through which his ascetic path takes him initially, does not ascend on the wings of the fancy of his mind, which keeps wandering about like a blind man, but proceeds towards the truth by the inexpressible power of the Spirit; spiritually and unfathomably he hears unfathomable words, he sees what is invisible, and already here on earth he is and becomes a miracle . . . he competes with the angels in incessant singing of praise to the Lord, he stands here on earth as an angel, leading all kinds of creatures through himself to God."[5]

Such are the incomprehensible spiritual experiences and lofty attainments of divine contemplation. Professor Archimandrite Cyprian explains their meaning as follows: "They demonstrate the possibility of overcoming the created world and the determinism of cosmic laws. A mystic leaves himself, the narrow framework of the created world, the laws of logical thinking, the category of time and space; he ascends to the third heaven, hears inexpressible words, is immersed in primordial abysses and is brought into contact with the transcendent foundations of creation. St. Dionysius writes that 'the soul aspires towards the incomprehensible light, unites with that which is above her, goes out of herself and becomes God's own.' "[6]

Summing up, we again quote Professor Archimandrite Cyprian: "Mystical knowledge is not only the knowledge of God and things divine, but also the

---

4. St. Simeon the New Theologian, *Homilies* (Moscow, 1892), Homily 90, pp. 487-489.
5. Archimandrite Cyprian, "Spiritual Predecessors of Gregory Palamas," in *Theological Thought (Bogoslovskii Mysl')* (Paris, 1942), pp. 129-130.
6. *Ibid.*, p. 108.

deification of one's mind; therefore mystical knowledge may apprehend God's mysteries about Himself, about the world, about man, about the beginning and the end of everything, about the things which remain out of reach for a theologian."[7] It should be also noted that mystical contemplations are not the experiences of certain subjective psychological states of joy, peace and repose; they are the revelations of another world, actual contact with this spiritual yet really existing world. It is only by the power of grace that man can attain such supernatural states. "Therefore," says St. Gregory of Sinai, "anyone who approaches contemplation without the light of grace should know that he is given to the fancies of his mind rather than contemplation, and that being in the power of fantasies he is deceiving himself."[8] And further: "Do not create fantasies yourself, and do not take in those that intrude upon you, and do not allow them to be impressed upon your mind. Because all the impressions coming from *without* and affecting our imagination serve to deceive the soul."[9] ". . . The mind itself possesses the ability to fantasize and can easily create illusory images of that which is desired. . . . Thus, a person experiencing this is a dreamer, and not a hesychast."[10]

A wonderful definition of hesychasm is given by St. Nicetas Stethatos (11th century): "Hesychasm is the state of mind unencumbered by thoughts. Stillness is freedom (from passions) and delight of the soul, the abiding of the heart in God, undisturbed and unwavering, intense contemplation, knowledge of divine mysteries, the word of wisdom coming from a pure heart, discourse with God, an unsleeping eye, mental prayer, effortless repose amid great efforts and, finally, union with God."[11]

Concluding our discussion on hesychasm, we will quote St. John of the Ladder: "Only those who have acquired divine consolation and encouragement in their efforts and divine help in the inner warfare are capable of true stillness."[12] In other words, hesychasm is not for everyone, but only for those chosen for it by God's grace. True ascetics never aspired to direct mystical contemplation. This would expose them to the danger of "deception." Exalted spiritual contemplation is not the lot of every ascetic, but only of a few giants of the spirit. "One out of thousands may attain to pure prayer, but hardly one out of ten thousand may attain to the state beyond pure prayer" (St. Isaac the Syrian).

---

7. *Ibid.*, p. 26.
8. *The Philokalia (Dobrotolubie)*, Vol. V (Moscow, 1900), p. 233.
9. *Ibid.*, p. 224.
10. *Ibid.*, p. 213.
11. *Ibid.*, p. 131.
12. St. John Climacus, *The Ladder*, Step 27:55.

In his excellent essay on the types of spiritual ascent, Fr. Paul Florensky[13] establishes an ontological differentiation of spiritual types and their hierarchy. Although every type may grow indefinitely in spiritual perfection along its "curve," the character of growth, abilities and spiritual endowment all vary. The groups of types within one "species" may surpass one another in the process of growth, both in speed and intensity; they may differ from one another infinitely, and yet one may establish a certain kinship or bond between them, and they may be compared. But the different kinds of "species" are simply beyond comparison. They are of another "dough," another substance. One "species" is characterized by the ability to soar high, being endowed with the wings of an eagle; another ascends along a gently sloping curve, and it may happen that a man does not have enough time to reach the heights of Divine contemplation, the time being limited by his life's span. The disciple of a correct spiritual school never sets contemplation as an object, but rather strives towards purification from passions. The rest depends on a person's ability to ascend spiritually, on his efforts in this direction, on a correct school and an experienced elder, if the latter can choose the shortest path for his disciple. However, seeing an ascetic's firm resolution and persistence, the Lord crowns him with the fruit of the Spirit.

Professor Archimandrite Cyprian develops the same idea: "Mysticism is, first of all, a special charisma of the Holy Spirit. Not every ascetic will be granted mystical illumination, but every mystic follows the narrow and sorrowful path of ascetic endeavor. Because of this, some less endowed ascetics have only moral purification (catharsis) as their spiritual objective, while others, with a more acute spiritual vision, look deep into the vast abyss of primordial spheres and beyond the created world; they overcome the power of the attraction of our created world and, seeing their own deified future state, they communicate with God. They have not only a theoretical awareness of the dogma of incarnation — 'the Word became flesh,' with all its consequences in the classical formula of St. Athanasius of Alexandria: 'God became Man, so that man might become god' — but they actually see this deification in their mysterious visions."[14]

---

13. Fr. Paul Florensky, "Concerning Types of Ascent," in *Theological Messenger (Bogoslovskii Vestnik)*, Vol. II (1906), pp. 530-568. St. Paul Florensky was canonized with the New Martyrs and Confessors of Russia in 1982 *(editor)*.

14. Comment: "The word 'mysticism' does not exist in the language of our Fathers; this concept is of Western origin and is best rendered by 'acquisition of the Holy Spirit, aspiration to charismatic disposition." Archimandrite Cyprian, "Spiritual Predecessors of Gregory Palamas," p. 3.

Chapter Five

CONTEMPLATION IN THE BIBLE AND IN PAGANISM

THE WORD *CONTEMPLATIO* ($\theta \epsilon \omega \rho i \alpha$) is derived from the word *templum* — a place with a wide view, from where augurs made their observations. *Contemplari* means an attentive observation by one's eyes or mind. $\Theta \epsilon \omega \rho \tilde{\omega}$ means to look, to examine, then to relfect, ponder, philosophize.[1] Human nature is endowed with the ability to contemplate and to communicate with God. The history of mankind as recorded in the most ancient book, the Bible, actually begins with the story of this ability, of man's communication with God. "The story from the Book of Genesis gives us an idea about the intimate relationship between Adam, Eve and God, which was interrupted by the Fall. When passing through Paradise God calls Adam, and Adam hides himself (Gen. 3:8). From that moment on, man can no longer bear the sight of God. However, man is drawn to the vision of which he has now become unworthy. From that time on, in the entire course of Biblical history, this tormenting conflict between man's most profound aspirations and his awareness of his own unworthiness is evident, even in the greatest friends of God. God both attracts and frightens them."[2]

Neither were the best people of the pagan world deprived of feeling for God, although there it manifested itself differently than among the Jews, who received their religion through divine revelation. This resulted also in the fact

---

1. *Dictionnaire de la Spiritualite*, Fasc. XIII (Paris, 1950), p. 1717.
2. *Ibid.*, p. 1654.

that "the Greeks, and Plato's disciples in particular, conceived God's transcendence in a metaphysical sense: as long as man is not free of matter, he cannot have any contact with the spiritual world; he differs too greatly from it to reach it. The Bible, however, confesses man's moral iniquity: God is holy, man is sinful. To see God is not physically impossible for him, but it is forbidden: one cannot see God and remain alive."[3]

Both Jews and pagans aspired to know God, as we are told by the Greek philosophers Socrates, Plato and others. Their mystical experience may be called natural, as distinct from the supernatural Christian experience. The difference between them is as follows. In Christian contemplation, God Himself acts and unites with a purified soul. This is a supernatural act, an act of mutual love between the Creator and His creation. No notion of divine love is given in natural contemplation. A non-Christian soul may have only a very vague idea about God; it is as if one were to touch an object in the dark without a chance of determining it. This kind of mysticism, in comparison with Christian mysticism, is like a shadow.[4]

Mystical perception of the supernatural world contains also the possibility of contact with the powers of evil. A man who is not purified by repentance, and whose spiritual vision is not illumined by passionlessness, cannot have the "gift of discerning spirits"; and if, moreover, he has mediumistic inclinations, he can easily arrive at the state of self-deception or *prelest* (spiritual delusion). The only true path to contemplation is the path of Christian asceticism.

3. *Ibid.*
4. *Ibid.*, pp. 1717, 1762.

Chapter Six

PRELEST

THE MAIN DANGER in the way of ascetic endeavors lies in the possibility of *prelest*.

Bishop Ignatius writes that "men of prayer are subjected to all kinds of delusion if *repentance* does not form the foundation of their prayer, if it has not become the soul and the *aim of prayer*. Anyone trying to join the wedding feast of the Son of God without the clean and bright wedding garment[1] prepared by repentance, but simply in rags, in a state of self-delusion and sin, will be thrown out into pitch darkness — into demonic delusion."[2]

Humility always accompanies sanctity. Sanctity is unthinkable without it. Professor Archimandrite Cyprian says: "The humility with which St. Simeon the New Theologian acknowledges his imperfection, and contritely confesses his past sins and falls, serves as a guarantee that his mystical experience is completely free of the element of *prelest* and spiritual pride. Ascetic literature abounds in warnings to novices not to yield to false visions and delusions, not to take an angel of darkness for an Angel of Light. St. Simeon warns against believing in all kinds of knocking noises, voices, intimidations, visions of sensory light, fragrances, etc., which tempt the awareness of an ascetic at the time of prayer. . . . Along

---

1. In ancient times, a king would send a special festive garment to those who were invited to his feast. In one of the Savior's parables, the wedding garment symbolizes the grace of the Holy Spirit which God grants to a true ascetic.

2. Bishop Ignatius Brianchaninov, *Works*, Vol. I, p. 135.

with humility, the mysterious bond with the Church protects mystics from falling into any false mysticism."[3]

All varieties of self-delusion or *prelest* are of two kinds. They are caused, firstly, by improper activity of the mind and, secondly, by improper activity of the heart (feeling). "The desire and aspiration to perceive spiritual visions by a mind unpurified of passions and unrenewed by the Holy Spirit is filled with pride and lack of discernment; the same pride and lack of discernment make the heart desire and aspire to delight in holy and divine experiences while still being incapable and unworthy of receiving them."[4]

The first kind of delusion, caused by the heating of the mind and imagination, frequently ends in mental derangement and suicide. The second kind is called "opinion," and it leads to such a tragic end less frequently because it deludes the mind but does not drive one to a frenzy. Nevertheless, it is just as ruinous: an ascetic who tries to awaken love for God in his heart and compels himself to experience delight and rapture while disregarding repentance, achieves just the opposite: "he enters into communion with Satan and begins to hate the Holy Spirit." "Opinion," in various degrees, is very widespread. "Anyone who does not have a contrite spirit and considers himself a person of virtue and merit, anyone who does not strictly adhere to the teaching of the Orthodox Church, but thinks freely according to his own opinion or a foreign teaching, is actually in this kind of *prelest*. The degree of deviation and the persistence in this deviation determine the degree of *prelest*. . . . "[5] In our fallen state, only one kind of feeling is admissible in the unseen worship of God: the feeling of sorrow for one's sins and sinfulness, one's fall and ruin, which is also called lamentation, repentance, contrition of spirit. . . . " *A sacrifice unto God is a broken spirit: a broken and a contrite heart, O God,Thou wilt not despise* (Ps. 50:17).[6]

Bishop Ignatius Brianchaninov tells of a characteristic case of *prelest* caused by the heated mind and imagination. An Athonite monk paid him a visit and said: "Pray for me, Father, I sleep a lot and I eat a lot." As he was saying this, Bishop Ignatius felt heat exuding from the monk. In order to learn about the spiritual state of the Athonite, Bishop Ignatius asked the monk to instruct him in prayer. "Oh horrors!" This monk began teaching him a method of "ecstatic prayer, utilizing the imagination." Later it turned out that the Athonite was completely unfamiliar with the teaching of the Holy Fathers on prayer. Bishop Ignatius continues: "In the course of our conversation I said to him:

---

3. Archimandrite Cyprian, "Spiritual Predecessors of Gregory Palamas," p. 113.
4. Bishop Ignatius Brianchaninov, *Works*, Vol. I, p. 144.
5. *Ibid*., p. 148.
6. *Ibid*., p. 145.

'Look, Elder, when staying in Petersburg, under no circumstances take lodgings in an upper story; be sure you stay on the ground floor.' 'Why so?' objected the monk. 'Well,' I answered, 'if angels should suddenly decide to take you up and transport you from Petersburg to Mt. Athos, and if they would take you from the upper floor, they could drop you down and you would die on impact; if however, they would take you from the ground floor and drop you, you would only be bruised.' 'Believe me,' answered the Athonite, 'many times when I stood praying, a vivid thought would come to me that angels would take me up and carry me to Mt. Athos.' It turned out that the Hieroschemamonk was wearing chains on his body, was hardly sleeping, was eating very little, and that he was feeling warmth in his body and had no need of warm clothes in the wintertime. Towards the end of our conversation I decided to suggest to the monk that, being an ascetic and faster, he should try the method taught by the Holy Fathers. They advise to keep the mind free of any dream-like fantasies and wholly and attentively immersed in the words of prayer, 'to enclose the thought within the words of prayer' (St. John of the Ladder, Step 28:17). The heart then usually sympathizes with the mind, feeling salutary sorrow for the sins committed, as St. Mark the Ascetic said: 'When the mind prays without distraction it afflicts the heart: *a broken and contrite heart, O God, Thou wilt not despise*' (Ch. 34, *Philokalia*, Part I). 'After you have tried this method,' I said to the Athonite, 'let me know about the fruit of your experiment; it is inconvenient for me to undertake such an experiment, considering my distracted way of life.' The Athonite agreed. A few days later he came and said: 'What have you done to me?!' 'What happened?' 'Well, as soon as I tried to pray enclosing my mind in the words of prayer, all my visions disappeared, and I can no longer return to them.' During our further conversation, I did not detect the kind of impudence and self-reliance which I noticed in him during our first meeting and which are usually noticeable in persons given to self-deceptions and imagining themselves to be holy or spiritually successful. The monk expressed his wish to hear my humble advice. When I advised him not to differ from others externally, for this leads to haughtiness, he took off his chains and handed them to me. A month later he came again and told me that he no longer suffered from heat in his body, that he was now in need of warm clothes and that he slept more. He told me that many monks on Mt. Athos, renowned for their holiness, use the method of prayer which he had previously practiced and instructed others in that method as well."[7]

7. *Ibid.*, pp. 140-142.

ELDER ANATOLE (POTAPOV) THE YOUNGER OF OPTINA
standing in front of the cell of Elder Ambrose. Elder Anatole
was personally known to the author, being the leading
Elder of Optina at the time the author went there.

From the Kontzevitch photograph collection.

Chapter Seven

ELDERSHIP

1. WHAT IS ELDERSHIP?

*Follow after charity, and desire
spiritual gifts, but rather that
ye may prophesy.... But he that
prophesieth speaketh unto men to
edification, and exhortation, and
comfort.* (I Cor. 14:1, 3)

THE APOSTLE PAUL enumerates three ministries in the Church, independent of the church hierarchy: apostles, prophets, teachers.

Immediately after the apostles stand prophets (Eph. 4:11, I Cor. 12:28).
Their ministry consists primarily of "edification, exhortation, and comfort"
(I Cor. 14:3). With this aim, and also for pointing out or warning, prophets also
predict future events.

Through the prophet, the will of God is immediately revealed; and therefore his authority is limitless.

The prophetic ministry is a special gift of grace, a gift of the Holy Spirit
(charisma). The prophet possesses a special spiritual vision — clairvoyance. For
him the boundaries of space and time are, as it were, set aside; with his spiritual
gaze he sees not only events that are occurring now, but also future events. He
sees their spiritual meaning; he sees the soul of man, his past and future.

Such a high calling cannot but be bound up with a high moral level, with
purity of heart, with personal sanctity. Sanctity of life, indeed, was required of

the prophet from the first period of Christianity: "He must have the manner of the Lord. From his manner may be distinguished the false prophet and the (true) prophet," says one of the oldest works of Christian literature, the *Didache* (*The Teaching of the Twelve Apostles*).[1]

The ministries enumerated by the Apostle Paul have been preserved in the Church in all ages. The ministries of apostle, prophet, and teacher, being independent, may be combined with the rank of bishop or priest.

The prophetic ministry, bound up with personal sanctity, has flourished when spiritual life in the Church was high, and has declined in decadent periods. Most brightly of all is it manifested in monastic eldership.

The influence of eldership extended far beyond the boundaries of a monastery's walls. Elders spiritually guided not only monks, but also laymen. Possessing the gift of clairvoyance, they edified, exhorted, and comforted everyone (I Cor. 14:3); they healed illnesses of soul and body, warned against dangers, indicated the path of life, revealed the will of God.

Being a direct continuation of the prophetic ministry, eldership appeared under this name and in this form only in the 4th century, together with the arising of monasticism, as its guiding principle.

2. THE MEANING OF THE COUNSELLING ACTIVITY OF ELDERS

> *As a ship which has a good helmsman*
> *comes safely into the harbor with*
> *God's help, so the soul which has a*
> *good shepherd, even though it has*
> *done much evil, easily ascends to*
> *heaven.* (*Ladder of Divine Ascent*)

The hardships of inner ascetic struggle, which aims at acquiring purity and dispassion, reveal the great significance of the counselling activity of elders.

---

1. K. Popov, *The Teaching of the Twelve Apostles* (Kiev, 1884). pp. 21, 36. Professor K. Popov, who wrote a special study on this document, attributes it to the end of the 1st century. Consequently, Apostle John the Theologian was still alive then, and perhaps other Apostles as well. Thanks to this document, we have found out much about the life of the Church of the First Christians. Personally, I have been searching for five years to form the concept of eldership, since in our contemporary theological literature there is no such thing. And finally I found the answer to my quest — although under a different name, not under the name of eldership — in the most ancient Christian document, *The Teaching of the Twelve Apostles*.

St. John of the Ladder says: "Those who rely on themselves and think that they have no need of any guide are deceiving themselves."[2]

"Without a guide one easily wanders from the road, however prudent one may be; and so, he who willfully walks the monastic path easily perishes, even though he may have all wisdom."[3] The same idea is expressed by St. Mark the Ascetic (4th century): "For the man who goes his monastic way willfully and without any guidance often stumbles and falls into many pits and snares of the devil; he frequently exposes himself to many dangers, not knowing what awaits him at the end. For many have endured great ascetic labors, much hardship and toil for God's sake, but because they relied on their own judgment, lacked discernment, and failed to accept help from their neighbor, their many efforts proved useless and vain."[4]

The erroneous ways of self-willed monks are caused, among other things, by the fact that the demons always try to present light as darkness and darkness as light, as the Apostle says: *For Satan himself is transformed into an angel of light* (II Cor. 11:14).

The monks Ignatius and Callistus instruct: "Most importantly, in everything you do, ask to be advised by your spiritual father in Jesus Christ; for in this manner, by the grace of Christ, the unbearable and the arduous become easy, and it will seem to you that you are rapidly moving along a gently sloping field."[5] In this instruction we find five signs of a sincere spiritual attitude of spiritual children to their elder and guide: "1) complete faith in him, 2) truthfulness: being truthful before him in word and deed, 3) not following one's own will in anything, but instead trying to cut it off (*i.e.*, doing nothing according to one's own wish and understanding, but always asking for the elder's advice in everything), 4) never objecting or arguing, since arguments are caused by one's pride and unbelief, and 5) complete and sincere confession of one's sins and the secrets of the heart" (revelation of thoughts).[6]

3. THE REVELATION OF THOUGHTS

The revelation or confession of thoughts, according to Bishop Ignatius Brianchaninov, "was in all probability instituted by the Apostles themselves"

---

2. St. John Climacus, *The Ladder*, Step 1:7.
3. *Ibid.*, Step 26:237.
4. "Letter to Nicholas the Solitary," in the book of St. Mark the Ascetic (Optina edition).
5. *The Philokalia (Dobrotolubie)*, Vol. V, p. 355.
6. *Ibid.*, p. 319.

(James 5:16) and was generally practiced in ancient monasticism, as is clearly evident in the writings of Sts. Cassian, John of the Ladder, Barsanuphius the Great, Abba Dorotheus, and, in a word, in all patristic writings on monasticism. However, an indispensable condition for practicing confession of thoughts is a monk who has been brought up in this practice and has attained a certain degree of spiritual perfection.

St. Cassian the Roman says: "It is beneficial to reveal one's thoughts to the fathers, not just to any father, but to spiritual elders esteemed not because of their venerable age and gray hair, but because of their discernment. Many men, carried away by the obviously old age of an elder, confessed their thoughts to him, but instead of being healed they suffered harm caused by the incompetence of their confessor,"[7] "for not everyone by any means can take upon himself the thoughts confessed to him" (Sts. Barsanuphius and John).[8] St. Ephraim the Syrian forewarns: "If you are not yet in a great measure inflamed by the Holy Spirit, do not aspire to hear other men's thoughts."[9] "A confessor must be burning with the fire of grace, so that this fire may scorch the wickedness of other men's thoughts and passions, and that grace and confession may not break but rather bind even more the chain of moral relations between him and the men making a confession. An elder called upon to hear confessions 'judges in accordance with the Spirit of God abiding within him.' "[10] "Father, tell me what the grace of the All-Holy Spirit will reveal to you, and heal my soul" (Palestinian Patericon)[11] — these are the words with which a repentant monk addresses the ascetic. The grace of the Holy Spirit was, namely, the power which imparted to an elder his inner authority to hear the confession of thoughts and to cure them.

This practice, according to Bishop Ignatius, "is of unusual benefit for the soul: no other single ascetic effort mortifies passions with such ease and power as this one. Passions retreat from the one who mercilessly confesses them."[12]

"Anyone concealing his thoughts is incurable" (Sts. Barsanuphius and John). "Do not hide your thoughts, confusions and suspicions. . . . It is over such a man who hides his bad or good thoughts that the demons rejoice (St. Isaiah). "Having rejected shame, we should always reveal to our elders everything that takes place in our heart" (St. John Cassian). "A wicked thought will weaken immediately after it is confessed. And even before the penance is imposed, the

7. Bishop Ignatius Brianchaninov, *Works*, Vol. I, p. 545.
8. Smirnov, "Confession and Repentance in Ancient Monasteries of the East," in *Theological Messenger (Bogoslovskii Vestnik)* (April, 1905), pp. 755-763.
9. *Ibid.*
10. *Ibid.*
11. *Ibid.*
12. Bishop Ignatius Brianchaninov, *Works*, Vol. I, p. 545.

abominable dragon flees, as if dragged out into the daylight from his dark underground cave by the courage of confession and now displayed in his disgrace" (St. John Cassian). "Base thought is the beginning and the root of transgressions; when it is concealed it turns into an act of darkness" (St. Theodore the Studite).[13]

The revelation of thoughts is the most powerful weapon in the hands of a spiritual father and elder. The author of these lines frequently witnessed the Elder of Optina Monastery, Hieroschemamonk Anatole (Potapov) receive confessions of thoughts from the monks. This scene created a very strong impression. Filled with concentrated attention and reverence, the monks would one after another walk up to the Elder. They kneeled when receiving his blessing, and exchanged a few short phrases with him. Some passed through quickly, others lingered a few moments longer. One could feel that the Elder treated them with fatherly love and authority. Occasionally he would resort to an external mode of treatment, like gently slapping the penitent monk on the forehead, probably to fight off obtrusive thoughts. All the monks left the Elder at peace and consoled. This would take place twice a day, mornings and evenings. Truly, life in Optina was unmarred by troubles, and all the monks had a kind, even tender disposition; some were cheerful, others deeply concentrated. One has to see with one's own eyes the result of the revelation of thoughts in order to understand its meaning fully. An ancient monk described in the following words the state of holy joy experienced by a man after he confessed his thoughts: "I was full of ineffable joy, feeling my mind purified of any sinful desires. I delighted in a purity which I cannot describe. The truth itself is the witness of this; I was fortified by firm faith in God and by great love. . . . I became dispassionate and bodiless, enveloped in God's enlightenment, having been created by His will" (Palestinian Patericon, II, pp. 95-96).[14]

St. Abba Dorotheus (†620), when teaching about the fear of God, told of the blessed state he attained when revealing his thoughts to his Elder: "I was free of any sorrows, of any anxieties. If some disquieting thought occurred to me, I would write it down on a tablet (because I was used to writing down my questions before attending to the Elder); and no sooner would I finish writing than I would feel benefit and relief, so great was the carefreeness and peace in me. Not understanding the power of virtue and having heard that *we must through much tribulation enter into the Kingdom of God*, I was worried that I had no sorrows. I revealed this thought to my Elder, and he said: 'Do not grieve, you have

---

13. Smirnov, "Confession and Repentance in Ancient Monasteries of the East," in *Theological Messenger* (March-April, 1905), pp. 459-470.
    14. *Ibid.*, p. 472.

nothing to worry about. Whoever is in obedience to the fathers enjoys freedom from cares, and peace.' "[15]

Bishop Ignatius Brianchaninov says that those monks who live by the rules of St. Nilus of Sora, who submit to the guidance of the Holy Scriptures and the writings of the Holy Fathers, and are in the habit of confessing their thoughts, may be likened to men who see and live, while those who disregard such a way of life are like blind men, like corpses.[16]

4. CHARACTERISTICS OF AN ELDER

In ascetic literature, when choosing a spiritual guide one is advised not to look for great endowments in him, for an ability to perform miracles, or a gift of prophecy, etc., but to choose one who is experienced in spiritual activity, who has personally attained purification of passions: for even a man of passions may possess spiritual gifts. . . . St. Macarius of Egypt said: "It happens that one may have grace, although his heart is not yet pure. That is why some men could not but fall: they did not believe that smoke and sin were abiding in them along with grace."[17]

Only a man who has successfully traversed the path of spiritual labor himself can lead others along this path.

An ascetic who has without a particular effort received the gift of grace because of the purity of his soul, which he has preserved since childhood, may not have the ability to guide others. Because he is not familiar with the ways of evil from his own experience, he does not know of the warfare against passions, and therefore he does not perceive evil in others. There were cases when such elders, being holy themselves, harmed their disciples and even "drove them into delusion."

In order to direct others, one needs the gift of discernment: "This art is half-way to sanctity" said the Optina Elder, Fr. Leonid. A true elder must have the gift of discernment.

Bishop Ignatius speaks of this gift as follows: "St. Cassian the Roman says that the Egyptian Fathers, among whom monasticism especially flourished and produced astonishing fruits, affirm that 'it is good to give spiritual direction and to be directed by those who are really wise,' and they state that 'this is a

15. "Instruction on Fear in Christian Reading," 1829, in the *Patrology* of Archbishop Philaret of Chernigov (St. Petersburg, 1882), no. 244.
16. Bishop Ignatius Brianchaninov, *Works*, Vol. I, p. 545.
17. St. Macarius of Egypt, *Homilies*, Homily 26:25, p. 205.

very great gift and grace of the Holy Spirit.' An indispensable condition of such submission is a spirit-bearing guide who by the will of the Spirit can mortify the fallen will of the person subject to him in the Lord, and can mortify all the passions caused by the fallen will as well. Man's fall and corrupt will imply a tendency to all passions. It is obvious that the mortification of a fallen will, which is effected so sublimely and victoriously by the will of the Spirit of God, cannot be accomplished by a director's fallen will when the director himself is still enslaved to the passions. 'If you wish to renounce the world and learn the evangelical life,' said St. Simeon the New Theologian to the monks of his time, 'do not entrust yourself to an inexperienced or passionate master, lest instead of the evangelical life you learn a diabolical life. For the teaching of good teachers is good, while the teaching of bad teachers is bad. Bad seeds invariably produce bad fruits. Every blind man who undertakes to guide others is a deceiver, and those who follow him are cast into the pit of destruction according to the word of the Lord: *if a blind man leads a blind man, both will fall into a hole* (Matt. 15:14). . . .' Those elders who take upon themselves the role of the ancient holy elders without having their spiritual gifts should know that their very intention, their very thoughts and ideas concerning the great monastic work of obedience, are false; let them know that their very outlook or way of thinking, their reason and their knowledge are self-delusion and diabolical *prelest* which cannot fail to give birth to a corresponding fruit in the person guided by them.

"If there is no good director available," continues Bishop Ignatius, "it is better for an ascetic to be without one altogether than to submit himself to an inexperienced one. . . . It is a terrible business to take upon oneself duties (of eldership) which can be carried out only by order of the Holy Spirit and by the action of the Spirit. It is a terrible thing to pretend to be a vessel of the Holy Spirit when all the while relations with Satan have not been broken, and the vessel is still being defiled by the action of Satan (*i.e.*, dispassion has not yet been achieved)! Such hypocrisy is terrible. It is disastrous both for oneself and one's neighbor; it is criminal in God's sight, blasphemous. . . . 'St. Poemen the Great ordered that a penitent should immediately break with an elder if living with him proved to be harmful to the soul' (Alphabetical Patrology). Evidently this meant that the elder in question was breaking the moral tradition of the Church. It is another matter when no harm is done to the soul, and one is only disturbed by thoughts, which are obviously diabolical. We must not yield to them. They operate just where we receive spiritual profit, which is what the demons want to snatch from us."[18]

---

18. Bishop Ignatius Brianchaninov, *Works*, Vol. IV, pp. 92-96.

An elder who has gained personal experience in the school of sobriety and mental prayer of the heart, who has thus mastered spiritual-psychological laws, and who has already personally attained dispassion, becomes capable of guiding a novice in his "unseen warfare" on the way to dispassion. He must be able to penetrate the very depths of the human soul, to see the very inception of evil within it, along with the causes of this inception, to diagnose a disease and find the precise method of healing it. An elder is a skillful spiritual physician. He must clearly see the "inner make-up" of his disciple, *i.e.*, the character of his soul and the degree of his spiritual development; he must possess the gift of discrimination and "discernment of spirits," because at all times he has to be dealing with evil which tries to transform itself into an angel of light. As a man who has attained dispassion, an elder usually has other spiritual gifts as well: those of clairvoyance, of miracle-working, of prophecy. . . .

In the highest degree of proficiency, as exemplified in St. Seraphim of Sarov, an elder attains complete and unrestricted freedom to manifest his activity, for not he, but Christ lives in him (Gal. 2:20); all his activity is in the Holy Spirit, and therefore always in harmony with the Church and its institutions.

Eldership is not a hierarchical rank within the Church; it is a special kind of sanctity, and therefore it may inhere in anyone. A monk without any clerical rank could be an elder, as, for instance, was the case with Fr. Barnabas of Gethsemane Hermitage at the beginning of his activity in spiritual guidance. A bishop, too, may be an elder: for instance, Ignatius Brianchaninov, or Anthony of Voronezh, the great contemporary of St. Seraphim. There were elders among priests as well: St. John of Kronstadt and Fr. George [the New Martyr] of Chekriak village. Finally, eldership can also be taken on by a woman, as for example the clairvoyant Blessed Parasceva Ivanovna, a fool-for-Christ of the Diveyevo Convent, without whose advice nothing was ever undertaken in that monastic community. [Also, abbesses and righteous laywomen can function as eldresses.]

Thus, to sum up, eldership is a special gift of grace, a charisma exercised under the direct guidance of the Holy Spirit, a special kind of sanctity. While all members of the Church are bound to submit themselves to the Church authority, no one is bound to submit to the authority of an elder. An elder never imposes himself on anyone; one always submits to him voluntarily. However, having once found a true, grace-inspired elder and having surrendered to him, the disciple should unreservedly obey him in everything and his advice must be followed, because through the elder God's will is being directly revealed to him. And such "monastic obedience" — in the form that was practiced in ancient monasticism — is called by Bishop Ignatius "a lofty spiritual mystery."[19] Also

---

19. *Ibid.*, Vol. I, p. 540.

to "inquire of an elder" is not required of anyone, but once one has asked for advice, one must follow it for the above reason.

If a contemporary ascetic can no longer find an experienced spiritual director, through no fault of his own but by reason of a complete absence of the latter, he nevertheless should not lose heart and leave his ascetic endeavor. According to the advice of St. Nilus of Sora, a monk of today must turn to the Scriptures and the writings of the Holy Fathers; he must not be alone in this, but seek the "counsel of the more proficient brethren, though at the same time comparing their counsel with Scripture."[20] To encourage ascetics in their difficult situation, Bishop Ignatius refers them to the advice of St. Isaac the Syrian: "A monk should not doubt that he will receive the gift of Divine grace, just as a son does not doubt that he will receive inheritance from his father. This inheritance is his by the law of nature." The aim of monasticism is renewal by the Holy Spirit, but St. Isaac names repentance and humility as the means towards this aim, and advises monks to acquire the ability to weep over themselves and use the prayer of the publican. He suggests that we uncover in ourselves enough of sinfulness to make our conscience remind us that we are but unworthy servants and in need of mercy. "Divine mercy," says the Saint, "comes to us by itself and at the time when one is not thinking about it. Indeed it is so — but only if the ground is pure and undefiled."[21]

We should repeat here that proper ascetic endeavor is impossible without the Jesus Prayer. Speaking of those who are afraid to begin practicing the Jesus Prayer, the Elder Basil Polyanomerulsky (the teacher of St. Paisius Velichkovsky) says: "Some who are unfamiliar with this prayer from their own experience think that they have the gift of discernment, and they justify themselves, or, you might say, are disinclined to learn this holy activity for three reasons or considerations. Firstly, they dismiss it as an exclusive feature of holy and dispassionate men. The second reason given is the scarcity of experienced guides and teachers, and the third reason — the danger of delusion. However, these reasons are ungrounded: the first — because the initial stage of spiritual progress for novices consists of the weakening of passions by sobriety of the mind and watchfulness of the heart, i.e., mental prayer, as it befits an active soul. The second argument is unreasonable and ungrounded because in the case of a lack of proper guides and teachers, Holy Scripture is our teacher. The third argument entails self-deception: instead

---

20. *Ibid*.
21. *Ibid*., p. 163 (St. Isaac the Syrian, Homilies 55 and 2).

of learning about delusion and the cautions against it from Holy Scripture, these cautions themselves are misinterpreted and presented as a basis for reluctance to practice mental prayer. If you fear to practice this prayer out of reverence and simplicity of heart, know that I, too, fear it for this reason — but not because of some senseless fables, according to which 'if you fear the wolf, don't go into the forest.' One should fear God, but not run away from Him or renounce Him on account of this fear."[22]

The contemporary position of spiritual guidance (*dukhovnichestvo*), as we will soon see, goes back to ancient monastic eldership (*starchestvo*) and is its secondary form. Because of the kinship of these two phenomena (spiritual guidance and eldership) many less experienced priests, only theoretically familiar with ascetic literature, may always be tempted to "exceed their authority," to overstep the boundaries of their position as spiritual guides, in order to assume the role of an elder, while in actual fact they do not understand what true spiritual counselling by elders is all about. This circumstance is fraught with the danger of causing irrevocable harm to the souls of their spiritual wards. It is well known that there have even been cases of suicide as a result of such harm being inflicted.

In pseudo-eldership, the will of one person is enslaved by the will of another, contrary to the point made by the Apostle Paul: *Ye are bought with a price, be not ye the servants of men* (I Cor. 7:23), and this situation entails a feeling of oppression, despondency or an unhealthy partial attitude to the "elder." A true grace-filled attitude to an elder, although based on unconditional obedience, does not deprive a person of the feeling of joy and freedom in God, because he is not in submission to the will of man, but through it to the will of God. He knows from his experience that the elder shows him the best way out of any given external difficulty, or offers him the best cure of his spiritual illness.

While the grace-filled elder is the bearer of God's will, the pseudo-elder overshadows God.

One should not confuse the counselling activity of elders with monastic discipline and the authority of superiors, or with the special kind of ascetic endeavor in which a monk submits to complete external obedience to a frequently severe and passionate "elder," thus consciously embracing martyrdom, as it were. Not every monk is strong enough to go through this kind of mortification of his will, and it may cause great anguish and indifference in the spiritual life. It is not an example to be imitated, but rather an exception worthy of astonishment.

Bishop Ignatius tells novices to obey the superior and other monastic authorities, as well as to obey "all fathers and brethren in matters that do not conflict with the Law of God, or with the rule and order of the monastery, or with

---

22. *Ibid.*, p. 128.

the directives of the monastic authorities. But on no account obey what is evil. . . . Seek the advice of virtuous and sensible fathers and brethren, but accept their advice with extreme caution and discretion. . . do not be carried away by advice which impresses you greatly at the start," for it may appeal to you because of your inexperience or because it gratifies some hidden passion within you.[23]

The relationship of an adviser to a learner entirely differs from that of an elder to a novice, a slave in the Lord, for whom the elder assumes complete responsibility. An adviser is not responsible for his advice if he has given it with the fear of God and with humility, not of his own accord but because he was asked and required to give it. And compliance with the advice received is not compulsory: it may be carried out or not carried out. "Let us not hide the word of God, but let us make it known," says St. Nilus of Sora. "The Divine Scriptures and the words of the Holy Fathers are as numerous as the sands of the sea. Diligently searching them out, we teach them to those who come to us and who are in need of them (who require them, ask for them). More correctly, it is not we who teach, because we are unworthy to do so, but it is the blessed and holy Fathers who teach from Divine Scripture." "There you have a superb model for our guidance today!" concludes Bishop Ignatius.

A certain experienced priest, speaking of spiritual guidance and pointing to the difference between the counselling activity of elders and that of spiritual guides, expressed himself as follows: "A spiritual guide directs one to the path of salvation, while an elder leads one along this path."

5. ELDERSHIP AND SPIRITUAL GUIDANCE IN HISTORY

The elements of eldership (*starchestvo*) can be found already in the charismatic phenomena of early Christianity. These charismatic phenomena, says Professor Smirnov, reappeared in ancient monasticism, and the elders were the bearers of the charisma — the special gift of the Holy Spirit, received by man directly from God for his personal achievement. The right to bind and to absolve, or the "power of the keys," was interpreted then as the highest and most perfect gift.[24]

---

23. *Ibid.*, Vol. IV, pp. 98-104

24. In ancient times, sacramental confession was not regarded as the only, exclusive and inevitable means for remission of sins committed after baptism. Confession and repentance were regarded as only one of many methods of purifying the soul from sins. St. John Chrysostom, for example, points out five such methods: 1) public confession, 2) weeping over sins, 3) humility, 4) charity — the queen of virtues, and 5) prayer.

Let us examine: What is this monastic practice? A spiritual father (πνευ-ματικός πατήρ)[25] does not mean a priest who follows a bishop's instructions; he is an "ordinary monastic elder, an indispensable guide of monks, independently appointed at a monastery and freely chosen by the pupil. For the most part, he does not have a clerical rank." "He would take his pupils' souls upon his own soul and, step by step, he would guide their spiritual lives, and, therefore, upon receiving their confession of thoughts and deeds, he would encourage and punish them."

The customary and moral relations between the elder and his pupil — spiritual father and spiritual son — both outwardly and inwardly, soon formed a solid and harmonious system which established itself as a monastic custom. The elder (as, subsequently, the spiritual father) would hear the confession and repentance, usually going over all sins, starting with a fleeting sinful thought slightly disturbing the monastic conscience, and ending with a mortal sin. "This confession and repentance before the elder used to replace the Church confession and repentance."

The influence of the elders amongst the laity began spreading very early, probably during the first years of monasticism. Laymen would seek out the elders, bypassing their pastors.

This discipline of monastic repentance in Church must have spread for reasons of its comparative ease, its superior quality and vitality, its "strictly pastoral character due to the presence of a superior and popular eldership, unavailable in the Church confessions."

For certain canonical sins, the ancient Church would first excommunicate the guilty person and then subject him to a public confession. The elder, however, upon hearing the brother's confession, would immediately reconcile him to his conscience and impose upon him a much lighter form of penance than the church would — thus he "bound and loosed."

Gradually, in the East, the monastic discipline of confession supplanted the church confession performed by the white (non-monastic) clergy, and the elders turned into father-confessors.

How did this happen? How did the monastic discipline become transformed into a general church discipline, while confession before an elder approached sacramental confession?

This phenomenon can be traced back to the Byzantine Church at the time of Leo the Armenian (†820) during the iconoclastic controversy, when the monastic elders were officially recognized by the Patriarch of Constantinople,

---

25. This term appeared already in the 4th century and existed until the first half of the 9th century.

Nicephorus the Confessor, along with his bishops and priests. This measure was caused by the needs of the time: Orthodoxy was in danger, and it relied on the cooperation of the most zealous defenders of the veneration of icons — mostly Studite monks. As a local measure, this paved the way towards supplanting the white clergy in the practice of confession throughout the Orthodox East and for a long time to come — and this was realized after the age of the Ecumenical Councils. In the course of the 10th to the 12th centuries, secret confession became predominant, having replaced public confession and canonical penances.

Thus, the "institution" of a spiritual father first appeared in the form of monastic eldership. The term "spiritual father" had for a long time denoted a monastic elder. Later this church custom, almost in its entirety, reappeared in the practice of spiritual father-confessors.

The monastic form turned into a customary form of the Church in general, and thus existed in the East almost unchanged throughout several centuries.[26]

When Christianity was adopted in Russia, the Greek and Bulgarian clergy brought their already-established discipline of repentance and the institution of spiritual father-confessors along with their customary features which had developed during the period of the Ecumenical Councils. This discipline existed in Russia almost untouched until the 18th century, since the ancient Russian Church authorities, being faithful to old traditions, showed hardly any innovation in this sphere.

The discipline of penance in the Slavic Churches differed somewhat from that of the Greek Church. Apparently, southern Slavs allowed the white clergy to be spiritual father-confessors, which was inadmissible in the Greek Church of that time.

It is possible that the remnants of the ancient Christian public discipline were not equally preserved everywhere.

Although Russia obtained the discipline of penance from Greece and Bulgaria, it deviated from their practice because of the great territorial expanse. A separate class of spiritual father-confessors soon ceased to exist, and every white (non-monastic) priest, upon ordination, acquired the right to hear confessions.

Another peculiarity of the Russian Church was that consequently the spiritual father-confessor became also a bearer of the priestly rank.

Now let us examine: what was this discipline? As was the custom of that time, everyone was free to choose his spiritual father-confessor, but once one had chosen him, one had no right to abandon him.

---

26. Smirnov, "Ancient Spiritual Guidance and Its Origin," in *Theological Messenger (Bogoslovskii Vestnik)*, 1906, Vol. II, pp. 369-382.

One was bound to obey him unconditionally, implicitly, and be loyal to him until the end of one's life. The spiritual father-confessor, on his part, assumed all the responsibility for the sins of his spiritual son and took his sins upon his own soul. Let us give an example of such taking on of sins: Having heard the confession and read the prayer over his bent-over repentant son, the spiritual father lifts him up from the earth and places his right hand on his own neck, saying, "Upon my neck are your sins, O child, and may Christ our God not punish you for them when He will come in His glory for His terrible judgment."

A spiritual father is not only the witness of his spiritual son's repentance before God, but is responsible, as it were, for his sins. The sin of a repentant son imparted to his spiritual father during confession became their common sin; they were accomplices in crime, as it were.

Being the surety of his flock, the ancient Russian spiritual father-confessor (*dukhovnik*) thus became a man's guide towards the New Jerusalem, who would open the Kingdom of God for him and lead him to God's throne, saying: "Here am I and the children which Thou hast given to me."

A spiritual father's power in guiding his spiritual children was to be unconditional and unlimited, like that of an abbot or the elder in a monastery, and the penance (*epitimia*) imposed by him had to be carried out as "the commandment of God"; and whatever he bound, he alone could absolve.[27]

27. Smirnov, *Ancient Russian Spiritual Father Confessors.*

Chapter Eight

SANCTITY

WE HAVE briefly discussed the path towards the acquisition of dispassion by means of "spiritual endeavor" — in other words, by sobriety, unceasing prayer, confession of thoughts, and obedience to an elder based on complete self-renunciation.

This "royal" path is the shortest; it leads directly to purity of heart and, consequently, to God-knowledge: *Blessed are the pure in heart, for they shall see God* (Matt. 5:8).

Dispassion is the fullness of virtue, the state of sanctity, because according to an immutable law, an eradicated passion is replaced by its contrary virtue.

Sanctity means purity of heart, the acquisition of grace (*i.e.*, of Uncreated Energy) both divine and deifying, which, like the many-colored rays of the solar spectrum, manifests itself in a variety of gifts of the Holy Spirit.

Sanctity is the fulfillment of hope, of faith and of love for God in His Spirit. The last gift, the gift of love, is the highest and most perfect gift, for even if a man should have the gift of prophecy, know all secrets, have all knowledge, and have faith to move mountains, but have no love, he is nothing (I Cor. 13:20). The highest knowledge of God, "gnosis," is bound up with the gift of love: *He that dwelleth in love dwelleth in God* (I John 4:16). St. Basil the Great says: "I am a man, but my task is to become god." This is accomplished in sanctity.

The fulness of God's grace, in transfiguring the holy struggler, overcomes the laws of created existence and the limits of time and space. Even the universal law of gravity loses its authority in view of the lofty concept of the unsubmissiveness of a saint to the elemental laws of this world.

The very damnation of God that has weighed heavily over man's pride since Babel — the confusion of tongues — loses its effect when, by way of the Holy Spirit, the gift of tongues is bestowed upon man.

The superabundant power of God reestablishes the original integrity of human nature when, through the remission of sins by a holy man, it heals also the bodily ills of a suffering person.

God's holy men form a visible link between our world and the Kingdom of Heaven, of God. They are truly angelic men and human angels. Ascending by degrees of perfection and becoming more and more imbued with the spiritual light of Divine grace, like red-hot iron in the fire, they become luminous like the sun when they have attained the highest state of deification through the mysteries, through contemplation of and communion with God.

Sanctity is inseparable from the Church, because the Church, being the mystical Body of Christ, is the *Way*, the *Truth*, and the *Life*. The Church is the way followed by all saints, and it is the truth in which they all abide.

There can be only one truth, since it is rooted in the one and only God. The perception of this truth — gained in the course of centuries through much suffering by way of collective endeavor — is the basic prerequisite for the acquisition of the grace abiding within the Church, Catholic and Apostolic.

And the Church, possessing the fullness of truth and the gifts of the Holy Spirit, offers them to all; but the world is unable to receive them by reason of its obduracy in sin and evil.

Mysticism is inseparable from Church dogmas. They are so closely bound that mysticism has its source in dogmas, and dogmas, in their turn, are supported by mystical experience. This is a familiar theme in theology. Vladimir N. Lossky says that "Eastern tradition never made a distinction between mysticism and theology, between personal attainment of divine mysteries and the dogmas established by the Church."

A century ago the great Orthodox theologian, Metropolitan Philaret of Moscow, illustrated this position to perfection: "None of the deepest mysteries of the divine economy should be regarded by us as alien, or completely transcendental: we should, in all humility, dispose our mind to contemplate divine matters." In other words, "dogmas express the revealed truth which to us appears as an unfathomable mystery, but which we must attain through a certain process. In this process, instead of assimilating the mystery according to our understanding, we should, on the contrary, abide by the profound change of our inner spirit, which would then prepare the ground needed to perceive spiritual matters. . . ." "Outside the truth presented by the catholicity (*sobornost*) of the Church, personal experience would be deprived of any trustworthiness, any objectivity. It would be a mixture of truth and lies, of reality and illusion — it would be 'mysticism' in the bad sense of the word."[1] Professor Archimandrite Cyprian, too, rejects the possibility of a personal spiritual experience outside the Church: "Along with humility, the mysterious bond with the Church protects mystics from falling into any false mysticism. No concoction of one's own, no self-assertion or setting up of one's personal experience against that of the Church is possible. A struggling ascetic verifies everything against his intuition developed in accordance with the teaching of the Church, taking the eucharistic life as the measure. The very nature of the Church is eucharistic. . . . True theological intuition is drawn from the depth of the Eucharistic Chalice, and it shines forth from the mysterious theurgical life. Abstract armchair philosophizing about God, outside the eucharistic life and without a living personal religious experience, namely the Church experience, is fruitless and therefore useless. Any daring attempts to force one's way into the sphere of mysticism without the eucharistic communion leads to nothing but self-deception, mystification of others and sectarian falling away from the Body of the Church."[2]

There are manifold types of sanctity, for the fullness of the Church of Christ embraces all life; the arches of the Church extend over the entire cosmos. Countless are the choirs of martyrs, followed by the choirs of monastic saints. The group of the Apostles is directly adjoined to the great teachers and Fathers of the Church, their work being continued by the hierarchs.

The most arduous feat (*podvig*) of self-renunciation has been accomplished by the "blessed ones" — fools-for-Christ. Having renounced their reason and the "wisdom of this world," they have taken up the cross of madness for the sake of the "madness of the Cross" (I Cor. 1:25), and received the highest spiritual wisdom instead. Any service in any walk of life performed in the spirit of self-renunciation and tor the sake of God, in prayer and sobriety, leads to dispassion, for all virtues are interconnected, and the attainment of one entails all the others.

Hagiographical volumes attest to this again and again. Thus, in ancient times we see St. Philaret the Merciful being filled with grace, although he conducted his life in a family circle and was the grandfather of an empress. Before us is the giant figure of St. Alexander Nevsky, a warrior-general, administrator and great benefactor and defender of his native land. We will not enumerate all

---

1. V. Lossky, *Essai sur la Theologie Mystique de l'Eglise d'Orient*, pp. 6, 11.
2. Archimandrite Cyprian, "Spiritual Predecessors of Gregory Palamas," p. 114.

the saints glorified in the world. There are many. Among them are princes, warriors, missionaries; there are youths, maidens and women who attained the state of sanctity.

The types of saints are endless and manifold. Every saint, even among those of the same type, has uniquely individual traits, for every person is unique: *And I will give him a white stone, and in the stone a new name written, which no man knoweth saving he that receiveth it* (Apoc. 2:17). However, what they all have in common is a moment of complete self-renunciation and resolve to follow Christ, a struggle undertaken for His sake in accordance with the Holy Gospel: *And he that taketh not his cross, and followeth after Me is not worthy of Me* (Matt. 10:38).

This is the only way; there is no other. Whoever strives towards high spiritual attainments but neglects the struggle (*podvig*) of self-renunciation for Christ, repentance and sobriety, he *climbeth up some other way* (John 10:1).

"The purpose of earthly life is the acquisition of the Holy Spirit," said St. Seraphim of Sarov. The grace of the Holy Spirit purifies, sanctifies and transfigures human nature. Man's will alone is insufficient to effect this, but without an effort on his part grace does not accomplish man's salvation: what is necessary is the cooperation (synergy) of man's free will and divine grace. The latter begins to work from the moment the ascetic (*podvizhnik*) enters the path of repentance and correct ascetic struggle (*podvig*); and like leaven it gradually penetrates the entire human nature, purifying and transfiguring it. Christ said: *Whereunto shall I liken the Kingdom of God? It is like leaven, which a woman took and hid in three measures of meal, till the whole was leavened* (Luke 13:20-21). St. Macarius of Egypt tells of such an effect of grace as follows: "Grace constantly abides, takes root and works like leaven in a man, and this abiding (of grace) within him becomes something natural, as if one with his being."[3]

Not everyone can attain spiritual heights, this "intense life of the saints." God does not demand sanctity from all, but He desires salvation for all. God's infinite love calls everyone to partake of the feast of His glory. The most modest worker who received only one talent and walked the path of his life in repentance and humility is welcomed *into his Father's arms*. It is never too late to enter the path of repentance: "If any has tarried even until the eleventh hour, let him also not be alarmed at his tardiness; for the Lord, Who is jealous of His honor, will accept the last even as the first; He giveth rest unto him who cometh at the eleventh hour, even as unto him who hath wrought from the first hour. And He showeth mercy upon the last, and careth for the first; and to the one He giveth,

---

3. St. Macarius of Egypt, *Homilies*, p. 69.

and upon the other He bestoweth gifts. And He both accepteth the deeds, and welcometh the intentions, and honoreth the acts, and praiseth the offering."[4]

"Salvation is effected between fear and hope" (St. Peter Damascene). Regardless of the heights attained by a holy man, he may always fall, but there should never be a place for despair.

"Even if you do not see anything good in yourself," said Elder Macarius of Optina, "or if you are a captive of sin, this should humble you rather than confuse you, because the state of confusion makes the feeling of contrition impossible. No sin can claim victory over God's mercy; repent, and He will accept your repentance, as He did that of a fornicator and a harlot." If you cannot repent, but commit sin because you are accustomed to it, and against your will, as it were, have the humility of the publican, and this should "suffice for your salvation." For a repentant sinner who does not give way to despair considers himself the worst of all creation and does not dare to judge or reproach anyone, but is in awe before God's love for humankind, is grateful to God and "may have other good things." Should someone obey the devil by committing a sin, but out of the fear of God disobey the enemy when tempted by him to despair, there is "the hand of God in this" (St. Peter Damascene). "And let no man allow his soul to be conquered (by deviating into despair), as long as he breathes, even if his boat should suffer battering daily." Herein lies God-given wisdom; and he is "a wise sick man" who does not cut off his hope (St. Isaac the Syrian, Homily 7). But what one should fear is to remain in sinful negligence in the hope of future repentance, because such an attitude is the same as despair.[5]

Of the five synonyms denoting "sanctity," the word ἅγιος was the most rarely used among the ancient Greeks, inasmuch as it was inaccessible to them.

In the Bible, however, both in the New and the Old Testaments, it is almost the only word which expresses the concept of sanctity "characteristic of the religion of the true Revelation exclusively, i.e., the concept in which the main principles and basic purpose of Divine Revelation are concentrated."[6]

In Christianity, the word "sanctity" is filled with a completely new, uniquely Christian content.

The pagan concept of sanctity denotes the outward relationship of a person or object to Divinity: dedication or belonging to it. The essential constituent,

---

4. *The Pentecostarion*: Paschal Homily of St. John Chrysostom.
5. *Letters of Hieroschemamonk Macarius of Optina to Laity* (Moscow, 1862), pp. 17-21.
6. Zarin, *Asceticism*, Vol. I, Book 2, pp. 17-21.

i.e., the chief moment, of the Christian concept is completely absent. The reason for this is that before the outset of Christianity, Divinity was not known as "love," which alone could call forth a real inner relationship between God and man, cause the inner transfiguration of man's nature and give his life a truly moral character.

In the pagan concept, the sanctity of Divinity was thought of as God's separation, His detachment from the world, His exalted position above everything, His infinity and incomparability to anything created. It was thought that God, being "holy," does not tolerate violation of the moral law. He punishes man for his conscious and unconscious crimes and vices, but He also does not tolerate man's outstanding moral perfection, which He regards as a desire to be His equal, as an infringement upon the divine prerogatives. Thus, an element of vindictiveness, of self-love, enters the divine life, essentially destroying the concept of sanctity.

According to the teaching of the Bible, however, man's "sanctity" consists of *his becoming like God*: the reflection and realization of divine perfection within man. Being the only bearer of the true and all-perfect, absolute life, God is also the one and only source of "sanctity." Hence, human beings may only be "participants" of His "sanctity," and this only by becoming partakers of His Divine nature. "For mankind which had sinned, such sanctifying communion with God became possible only in Christ, through the power of His redeeming sacrifice. This sacrifice was the precise and perfect fulfillment of God's will for the salvation of man, that he *should be holy and without blame before Him in love* (Ephes. 1:4)." With this purpose the entire Divine Revelation concerning the salvation of man is imbued.

The character of divine sanctity was such that it excluded the possibility of God's communion with sinful peoples. This is why one particular people was chosen from among all the nations of mankind to form a "holy" people, "for the purpose of making possible genuine union between God and man, which would be of significance for all of mankind."

Therefore, special demands of sanctity were made of the chosen people. The whole people had to be "holy" in conduct, because holy was the Lord, Who had chosen His people for a special destiny and Who had become closely bound to them in the communion of love.[7]

---

7. *Ibid.*

PART II

ANCIENT EASTERN
MONASTICISM

And they that are Christ's have crucified the flesh with its affections and lusts (Gal. 5:24).

A monk is an angel, and his work is mercy, peace and the sacrifice of praise
(St. Nilus of Rossano, †1005).

ST. ONUPHRIUS THE GREAT
(See p. 169).

The main icon of him in the St. Onuphrius Monastery in Poland.

Introduction

The Hierarchical Nature
of the Spiritual World
and the Place of Monasticism in It

HRISTIANITY WAS BORN amidst persecutions and sufferings. At any moment a believer had to be prepared for martyrdom. This put the greatest strain on his spiritual energy and renunciation of the world. Christ's commandment, *Let him deny himself, and take up his cross and follow Me* (Matt. 16:24), was fulfilled literally. Such a state of dispassion and sanctity was the lot of the elite, a few chosen ones.

Three centuries of persecution ended with the glorious triumph of Christianity over paganism. This heroic period was replaced by "the period of well-being and peaceful life." Religion became the property of the masses, and at the same time the high standard of early Christianity began to decline inevitably and fatally.

The new era required new methods of "attaining heavenly crowns."

In order to renounce the world, one now had to leave it; in order to attain dispassion, one had to follow the long path of "inward activity." Forced martyrdom was now replaced by voluntary mortification: self-denial and asceticism, the life of labor and deprivations in the desert.

The great exodus into the desert was about to begin; the era of monasticism was born. It was not in vain that monasticism became known as the "angelic way." "Angels are the light of monks, and monastic life is the light of all men." These brief words of St. John of the Ladder (†605) contain the idea expounded by St. Dionysius the Areopagite of the unity and hierarchical nature of both the visible and invisible worlds.[1]

The teaching about angels as secondary lights is generally widespread in all the Eastern patristic writings. Professor Archimandrite Cyprian tells us of the essence of this teaching:

The Holy Trinity is the Essential, Eternal and Uncreated Light. The essence of Divinity is unfathomable, but God, in His love for the world and man, incessantly pours out His Divine Light upon the created world. It is only in this outpouring of light, in this Divine Energy, the intelligent, uncreated and eternal Light of Mt. Tabor, that God may be perceived by angels and men. St. Dionysius the Areopagite calls it "God's appearance." St. Gregory Palamas approves of St. John Damascene's term "God's aspiration." This process of divine life in the universe proceeds gradually and within the framework of a strict hierarchy. The first to partake of this Essential Divine Light are the highest ranks of angels, and they pass it on in the hierarchical order of descendancy to the lower ranks of angels. They are like mirrors reflecting this Light. They are the "secondary lights."

After the angels, the most spiritually sensitive and gifted human beings are honored by the outpouring of light. Thus is formed the "golden chain" which, according to St. Simeon the New Theologian, "is firmly established in God and is unbreakable." St. Maximus the Confessor says that "created beings partake of the divine bliss according to their capacity," and in greater or lesser degree, depending on their merit. Thus, the world of angels is an intermediary between God and man.

On earth it is the monks who continue the "golden chain," linking man to the celestial world of angels, and spreading the light of sanctity, love and wisdom upon the earthly, corruptible, and fallen world. Monks must be imbued with this light and refract it in purity, mercy and the knowledge of God; they must continue and complete the task of the angels here on earth and become the "attending spirits" for those who are to inherit salvation, for humanity that languishes in sins and unbelief.

Monks may become like angels only in their spirit, not in their body: only in that "divine spark" within themselves, or, according to St. Gregory the Theologian, in their hypostatic principle. Their task, like that of any intelligent, spiritually endowed man, is to reveal the "potentially divine element" within

---

1. St. John Climacus, *The Ladder*, Step 26:31, p. 181.

themselves, to develop their spiritual endowment, to perfect themselves and approach the Divine Primary Source of life.

They can serve the world either by means of direct contact with it or by being desert-dwellers, anchorites. Being removed from the world geographically, the latter become even more closely bound to it metaphysically and spiritually through their prayer. Hermits leave the worldly life for the sake of the life of the world, for devotional service to the whole world, that they might protect it spiritually.

The motives of monasticism are not and have no right to be selfish. This would mean breaking the "golden chain," violating the universal unity of all members of the body of Christ, and falling away from the general plan of Divine Providence with regard to the world and man. Also, asceticism may not be regarded as an end in itself — it is only a means, moreover a negative means, manifested in abstinence and disregard of the lowly psycho-physical needs of man. The monastic vows of non-acquisitiveness and virginity are of the same negative nature. The purpose of monasticism, as a moral power, is not only to attain salvation for the monastics themselves, but also to save the whole world, and to attain the sanctification of creation. This is not only being saved *from* the world, but precisely saving the world. Therefore, without being repulsed by its sicknesses and without having an aversion to its uncleanness, monasticism serves the world: it protects it, prays it out of trouble, nourishes it, cleanses it through confession, and intercedes for it. To this aim was directed the service of a multitude of Holy Fathers, both those dwelling in the deserts and those revealing themselves to the world. Whether they raised themselves upon a pillar (as Sts. Simeon, Alypius, Nicetas and Daniel the Stylites) or placed themselves upon a rock (as St. Seraphim of Sarov), or fled into reclusion in deserted caves or forest sketes — all these were cases of intercession for the world. However, these ascetic endeavors and prayerful intercessions before the throne of the Lord were modified whenever the ascetics left their seclusion to serve their fellow men. It was usually the spiritually mature ascetics who would devote themselves to the task of ministering with compassionate love to their fellow men, addressing them with healing prayer and counsel. With the red-hot coal of God's Name, they touched the sores of the soul. They are the "merciful hearts"[2] of which St. Isaac the Syrian speaks in profoundly moving words, the hearts trembling with grief and compassion for every soul, for every creature, even for the enemies of the truth, *i.e.*, the demons. The line of these holy men goes back to ancient times, and extends to St. Paisius Velichkovsky and our own famous Elders of Optina. "Optina was one of the

---

2. St. Isaac the Syrian, *Ascetic Homilies* (Moscow, 1858), p. 299.

ST. GREGORY PALAMAS
holding an icon of the symbol of his teaching,
the Transfiguration of our Lord on Tabor.

A contemporary Russian icon.

most wonderful flowers of the monastic garden, one of the brightest lights of the
Orthodox world and of its angel-like choirs of monastics. Confession, guidance
and counsel of even the seemingly most prosaic nature drew the monks ever
closer to their objective — to be the guardian angels of the world.[3]

_____

3. Archimandrite Cyprian, *Angels, Monastics and Man* (Paris, 1942), p. 7.

Chapter One

THE HOLY FATHERS ON THE
ORIGIN OF MONASTICISM

WHILE IN THE MOLTEN STATE, crystalline substances have no distinct form; their particles float freely. It is only in the process of cooling that the distinct and clear forms of the crystal are developed. Similarly in the Church, her life, dogmas, canons and institutes at first do not have any clearly expressed forms. Only subsequently do they emerge out of the spiritual essence of the Church, according to the laws of truth contained in her bosom.

Thus, while the Church is in the molten state, as it were, and is permeated with the light and warmth of the Holy Spirit, any manifestations of life within her cannot be essentially untrue, because these manifestations lie in the Holy Spirit and are moved by the Holy Spirit.

As the Church expands, she absorbs elements which are still in the initial phase of spiritual development, and which have not as yet overcome "the old man" (Adam). Due to these added new elements, deviations "to the right and to the left" become inevitable. The Church is aware of the falsity of these deviations; they compel the Church to express essential truth in order to give it shape and symbol, and place it within precise limits.

Thus the forms are crystallized, the Church becomes established and her entelechy affirmed.

This idea is confirmed in the Gospel. The Savior compares *the Kingdom of heaven . . . to a grain of mustard seed, which is the least of all seeds: but when it is grown, it is the greatest among herbs and becomes a tree, so that the birds of the air come and lodge in the branches thereof* (Matt. 13:32).

The seed of any plant potentially contains the whole plant, and with its growth nothing new or uncharacteristic of this plant is added to it. Thus, for example, nothing but an oak tree will ever grow out of an acorn. Similarly, Christianity from its very outset contained all its components, and the history of Christianity is only the further development of these components.

Thus, both monasticism and eldership must have existed, if only in embryonic form, from the very beginning of Christianity. The desert-dwellers considered St. John the Baptist as the founder of anchoretic monasticism. St. Innocent, a disciple of St. Nilus of Sora, wrote in his will: "If God will give His blessing for the church to be built in our desert, let it be established in commemoration of the great Saint, John the Baptist, on the feast day of the third finding of his venerable head, for he is the great teacher of all desert-dwelling monks." (For this reason the main church in the Optina skete was also dedicated to this Saint).

The aim of desert-dwellers is to acquire the gift of unceasing prayer. St. Gregory Palamas (†1360) elevated the practice of unceasing prayer to inaccessible heights, pointing to the Most Holy Virgin Mary as the first one to embrace unceasing prayer. He writes that the Most Holy Virgin Theotokos, while staying in the Holy of Holies and heeding Scripture, was filled with pity for fallen humanity and began Her quest for the best way to converse with God, to gain permission to intercede for humanity and ask for God's mercy. Looking for that which was most necessary, for prayer, and seeking that which awakens prayer, the Most Holy Virgin found the answer in the sacredness of stillness: stillness of the mind, remoteness from the world, oblivion to everything earthly, and ascent to divine contemplation. Abiding in stillness, the inner man is freed of all earthly, lowly, human concerns. He becomes estranged from the world and ascends to God. Remaining in prayerful devotion day and night in all stillness, man purifies his heart, becomes inexpressibly united with God, and sees God within himself as in a mirror.

Therefore the Most Holy Virgin Mary renounced all worldly concerns, rejected all communication with people and love for earthly pursuits, and chose a life invisible to all, remaining within the walls of the church. There she recollected her mind in an uninterrupted watchful abiding in God, and with the help of unceasing prayer rose above all worldly confusion and thoughts. Thus she walked a new ineffable path to heaven, which is the stillness of the mind. Rising above all created life, the Most Holy Virgin was able to contemplate God's glory much more clearly than was Moses. Having partaken of the divine grace beyond description and comprehension, she became the "bright cloud of living waters, the dawn of the conscious day, the fiery chariot of the Word."[1]

The solitary way of life of an anchorite is in contrast to another kind of monastic life, that of a coenobium (communal-type monastery).

According to St. John Cassian the Roman, an ancient writer of the end of the 4th century, the early Christian community was the prototype of the coenobium. **St. John Cassian** (†435), the son of rich and noble parents, received an excellent scholarly education. When still a young man, he went to Palestine and became a monk in a coenobitic monastery in Bethlehem. Having spent two years there, together with his friend Germanus, around the year 390 he decided to visit monasteries in Egypt, which were famous for their great ascetics. "Visiting all the renowned monasteries in Lower and Upper Egypt, like bees they gathered the best of what they observed in the monastery rules and in the lives of austere ascetics, and entered into discussions on various spiritual matters with the more enlightened and experienced elders."[2] Thus, St. John Cassian the Roman preserved for posterity his observations of monastic life in the early years of its development. These observations are of great value to us, because they reflect the life and views of the monks of that time. St. Cassian the Roman says that "this coenobitic type of life goes back to Apostolic times, since the majority of believers in Jerusalem adhered to it." In the Acts of the Apostles we read: *And the multitude of them that believed were of one heart and of one soul: neither said any of them that ought of the things which he possessed was his own; but they had all things common. . . . Neither was there any among them that lacked: for as many as were possessors of lands and houses sold them, and brought the prices of the things that were sold, and laid them down at the Apostles' feet; and distribution was made unto every man according as he had need* (Acts 4:32, 34, 35). – "such, I say, was the Church then," and such a way of life now is "very rare and hardly to be found even in coenobitic monasteries." "After the Apostles died, believers became less fervent, especially those from among foreigners and other nations, by reason of their old ingrained pagan customs." It was charitably demanded by the Apostles that they *abstain from meats offered to idols and from blood and from things strangled and from fornication* (Acts 15:29). When, however, the number of believers greatly increased because of the daily addition of new converts from "both the indigenous population and foreigners," this tolerance shown towards the former gradually began to weaken

---

1. Schemamonk Metrophanes, *The Life and Writings of the Moldavian Elder Paisius Velichkovsky* (Moscow, 1947), pp. 207-211. [English translation under the title *Blessed Paisius Velichkovsky* (Platina, California: St. Herman Brotherhood, 1976).]

2. *The Philokalia (Dobrotolubie)*, Vol. I.

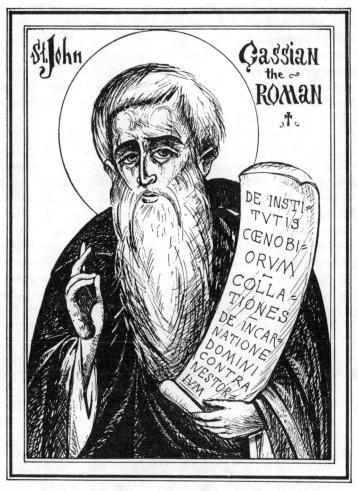

The scroll reads:

DE INSTI-
TVTIS
CŒNOBI-
ORVM
COLLA-
TIONES
DE INCAR-
NATIONE
DOMINI
CONTRA
NESTOR-
IVM

ST. JOHN CASSIAN THE ROMAN

A contemporary iconographic sketch by Gleb Podmoshensky.

the piety of the church of Jerusalem and to diminish "the fervor of the initial faith." It was not only the new converts "but also representatives of the Church who deviated from the former strictness." "For there were some who thought that things permissible to (former) pagans due to their weakness, were permissible to them as well, and that they would suffer no harm by keeping their property and their wealth, provided they kept their faith and confessed Christ."

Those, however, who preserved the zeal of early times began to avoid communicating with their indolent and dissolute fellow men. They left the cities for the more remote isolated places where they could practice "on their own" what the Apostles had instructed the entire Church to observe. Gradually, in time, they separated from the general mass of believers, because they avoided marriage and refused to participate in their parents' lives and in worldly social life in general. They began to be called monks, i.e., men living alone in strict solitary isolation. If they lived in a community, they were called coenobites, and their cells and places of dwelling were known as coenobiums. "Consequently, this type of monk was the oldest and the first, not only in time, but also in grace; as a type it remained intact for many years until the time of St. Paul of Thebes and St. Anthony the Great" (St. John Cassian).[3]

Thus the ancient Father St. John Cassian the Roman (4th century), and later St. Gregory Palamas (14th century), determined that monasticism originated in the days of early Christianity.[4]

---

3. Writings of St. John Cassian the Roman, in The Philokalia (Dobrotolubie), pp. 498-500.

4. For example, St. Mark the Evangelist lived in a celibate community in Alexandria, which continued for centuries after him (editor).

ST. PACHOMIUS THE GREAT
receiving the monastic Schema and Rule from an angel.

A fresco from the Great Meteora Monastery, Greece,
painted by Theophanes the Cretan (1527).

Chapter Two

A BRIEF HISTORICAL SURVEY OF ANCIENT EASTERN MONASTICISM

IT WAS FROM THE BEGINNING of the 4th century that monasticism began to develop. There were instances of individual hermits leaving cities even before that time, as, for instance, under Emperor Decius (249-251), when they hid from their persecutors in deserts, caves and underground pits. But these instances were exceptions rather than the common practice. Although many believers led an isolated kind of life in the cities, "monks did not yet know of the Great Desert," as St. Athanasius the Great stated.

The longing for the monastic life, the resettlement into the desert, began during the reign of St. Constantine the Great. At first it took place in Egypt, where two forms of monastic life coexisted from the start: that of the hermits and that of the coenobites. The first guide of ancient monasticism was **St. Anthony the Great** (born 251). For a long time he lived the life of a hermit in austere seclusion in the desert, close to the banks of the Nile. His followers began seeking him out, desiring to be instructed by him. He kept refusing, but finally gave in to their request and permitted them to settle in the neighborhood and build "monasteries," *i.e.*, single cells similar to the tents of nomadic tribes. These, then, were the first colonies of hermits. They lived separately, as far as possible avoiding communication among themselves, in complete seclusion; nevertheless they formed a "brotherhood" united through spiritual guidance.

Similar settlements arose in the Nitrian desert around **Abba Amoun** (died between 340 and 345), and in their vicinity were established other settlements known as "kellia" (cells). Still further away in the desert were established "sketes" (in Coptic *sheet* — great valley). The "kelliotes" lived separately in concealed cells. These are the same as recluses. "A man who has learned of the sweetness of a cell avoids his neighbor" (St. Theodore of Pherme). "Until a man say in his heart: I alone and God exist in the world — he will find no repose" (Abba Alonius). This solitary way of ascetic endeavor is arduous, and for many even dangerous. Very early there came into existence another type of monastic settlement, where monks lived as a community: the coenobium.

The first coenobium was established by **St. Pachomius the Great** (born 292), who began his ascetic struggle as a hermit. He realized that the solitary way of life was too difficult for novices and did not benefit them. One had to be gradually brought up and prepared to embrace the creative freedom of anchorites (hermits). St. Pachomius organized in Tabenna a communal life on the principles of strict obedience. The whole life in their monastery was to be based on faithful observance of set rules, even in the smallest matters, with the cutting off of one's will (self-will). Instead of the creative improvisation of solitaries, here the monks were to realize the idea of a well-measured life protected by a severe discipline of supervision and penalties. Anchorites were usually milder and more condescending towards their weak brothers and sinners. St. Pachomius' monastery was an educational institution; even those ignorant in matters of faith were admitted. The purity and steadfastness of the candidates' intentions were subjected to a severe trial. One of the elder brethren would be appointed to guide a beginner. Monks lived in separate houses, about forty of them, supervised by a director. They would all come together for prayer. Handicrafts were assigned according to strict instructions. No one was allowed to do less or more, or wilfully to change them. It was a shared life, shared work, carried out with mutual concern, with no secrets harbored. Tradition has it that the Lord's Angel who gave St. Pachomius his monastery's Rule said: "The Rule is for those whose mind is not yet mature, so that remembering the Rule of common life, in fear before the Lord, they might attain freedom of spirit, be they even unruly slaves." Both coenobites and anchorites have a common ideal — "freedom of spirit" — but the path to it is now different [with coenobitism].

St. Pachomius himself founded nine coenobitic monasteries. Their common abbot lived in Tabenna, and later in Pevou. In St. Pachomius' lifetime, communal monasteries were springing up throughout Egypt. His sister organized a coenobitic monastery for women. In the vicinity of Atripa the hermit Bgul founded the "White Monastery," the long-time Abbot of which was the fierce and severe Shenouda. Its Rule was very strict and included corporal punishment. Characteristically, those who passed the test of community living acquired the right to live in seclusion; however, it was demanded of them that they assemble four times a year in their original monastery.[1]

One of the successors of St. Pachomius the Great was **St. Theodore the Sanctified** (291-348). Whereas St. Pachomius tried to motivate the brothers to repent by portraying the terrible lot of sinners, St. Theodore would try to awaken hope rather than fear. History has preserved for us a vivid description of the brothers' revelation of thoughts before St. Theodore:

"There were six hundred brothers assembled. . . . An amazing order prevailed in such a numerous gathering of monks. One after another the brothers would rise and walk up to Theodore, asking him to reveal their shortcomings before all those present. Theodore would quote from Holy Scripture a passage relevant to the state of each individual brother. They would then return to their places with contrite hearts and in tears. It was not only by his experience and knowledge of his monks' inner states that Theodore was able to find suitable words from Scripture for each one of them, but rather by a supernatural knowledge which God revealed to him about their souls. His experience of this spiritual clairvoyance would manifest itself in his prophecies concerning the future destiny of the Church. Thus, a certain monk walked up to him, as had other brothers before him, when suddenly they noticed that Theodore fell silent, gazed up to the sky, then rose from his seat. All the brothers rose, too, and formed a circle around their Elder, realizing that he was about to give them some important instructions."[2]

And indeed, St. Theodore foretold to them events which soon came to pass. Namely, he told them about the exile of St. Athanasius the Great, about the dominations of the Arians, the enthronement of Julian [the Apostate], then Julian's death and the enthronement of Jovian, who brought peace to the Church. These prophecies concluded the session of the "revelation of thoughts" — the scene of which was described by its witness, St. Amoun.

"This Amoun has made the mountain of Nitria famous." There lived also **St. Pambo**, about whom St. Anthony said that the Spirit of God dwelt in his heart. According to St. Pambo, obedience to an elder is superior to non-acquisitiveness and great love, because these latter virtues are acquired voluntarily, whereas a monk under obedience renounces his own will and fulfills the will of another man. Renunciation of one's will is the highest sacrifice of man, surpassing all other sacrifices.

---

1. Florovsky, *Byzantine Fathers of the 5th to 8th Centuries* (Paris, 1933), pp. 140-143.
2. Professor P. Kazansky, *History of Orthodox Monasticism in the East* (Moscow, 1854), pp. 205-206.

In the desert of the cells, **St. Macarius of Alexandria** (295-395) and **St. Macarius of Egypt** (born 300), called the Great, were well known. Generations of ascetics of all ages were brought up on the writings of St. Macarius the Great and his school. He was once asked: "Tell us, what degree of spiritual perfection have you reached?" He replied. "Now after the sign of the cross, grace imbues the entire body and heart with peace. The soul is full of great joy, like an infant who knows of no evil, and the man no longer judges another man, be he a Greek or a Jew, a sinner or layman. He looks upon all of them with the pure eye of his inner being; he rejoices over the whole world and wishes to respect and to love both the Greeks and the Jews. At another time he, the King's son, firmly places his trust in the Son of God, as his father. Doors open before him, and as he enters, numerous doors open before him again — a hundred mansions leading to a hundred beyond. And the richer he becomes, the more new wonders are shown to him. He, being the son and heir, is entrusted with things which no human being is able to express or utter with his tongue. Glory be to God. Amen."[3]

"It should be noted," says Professor Archimandrite Cyprian, "that from his mystical experience St. Macarius knew what path all Eastern mysticism would subsequently take. St. Macarius was one of the first hesychasts. His instructions on the struggle with passions, on purification of the heart, on freeing the mind, *i.e.*, on its sobriety, all pursue the main objective: man's illumination. The mystical teaching of light, which is attained by quieting the mind from everything that may disturb and exasperate it, was well known to this desert-dweller of the 4th century, one thousand years before St. Gregory Palamas and the hesychasts came out with their teaching on the subject. Their very term 'hesychia' (stillness) was frequently used by him in association with the concepts of 'peace,' 'calming down,' 'prayer,' 'silence,' etc. Hesychasm was in no way an 'innovation' or 'invention.' St. Gregory of Sinai gave an even clearer and more precise definition of what the ascetics of the 4th century knew from experience."[4]

Elder Macarius of Optina also spoke of spiritual labor, or inward prayer, as an ancient practice. Not all the ascetics were familiar with both the concept of inward prayer and its outward, bodily methods. Thus, at the time when the Sinai ascetics practiced it, the Athonite monks observed only "active piety." The Holy Fathers of the first centuries, even if they spoke about the form of inward prayer, did so rather vaguely, in order not to cause harm to unbelievers or brazen

---

3. St. Macarius of Egypt, *Homilies*, p. 71. St. Seraphim of Sarov was totally imbued with the teaching of St. Macarius. In his conversation with Motovilov he expounded on the parable of the five wise and five foolish virgins in accordance with the interpretation of St. Macarius, who had explained this parable twice in his writings.

4. Archimandrite Cyprian, *Anthropology of St. Gregory Palamas*, p. 223.

men who follow their self-will. Thus, St. John of the Ladder wrote (Step 27): "Let the remembrance of Jesus be present with each breath, and then you will know the value of stillness." And St. Simeon the New Theologian spoke of St. Anthony the Great: "What would he have done when dwelling in the dark pagan tomb, if he were not familiar with the form of inward prayer?"[5]

Towards the end of the 4th century, Egypt was covered with monasteries. From there monasteries moved into Palestine. Already in the 20's of the 4th century, the first anchoretic monastery was established near Gaza, around the cell of St. Hilarion, a disciple of St. Anthony the Great, and nearby was established the monastery of Epiphanius, who subsequently became the Bishop of Cyprus. Later were established "lavras" ($\lambda\alpha\acute{\upsilon}\rho\alpha$ – a narrow passage, street), or large coenobiums. The first lavra, Faran, was of St. Chariton near Jerusalem; and then other lavras sprang up along the way from Jerusalem to Jericho, and around Bethlehem. St. Euthymius organized his monastery in the 5th century, and in the 6th century St. Sabbas the Sanctified founded his monastery with a lenient coenobitic rule, where life in a community was regarded as a preliminary step towards the anchoretic life.

The principle of communal life was described in the 4th century by St. Basil the Great. His coenobitic rule was of great influence throughout the history of monasticism, not only in Byzantium but in the West as well.

Monasticism in Syria developed independently of its Egyptian counterpart. Many monasteries were founded there around big cities. Characteristically, the Syrian monks were known to have practiced self-mortification. There were ascetics in the 6th century who were called "grazers" ($\beta\acute{o}\sigma\nu\sigma\iota$), and later there were stylites.[6]

Among Syrian ascetics were two great figures who shone forth: St. Ephraim the Syrian (4th century) and St. Isaac the Syrian (7th century). St. Ephraim was a prophet and a scholarly writer, and he was endowed with an outstanding lyrical talent. Everyone is familiar with his prayer: "Lord and Master of my life. . . ." St. Isaac the Syrian refused to become a bishop and spent all his

---

5. *Letters of Hieroschemamonk Macarius of Optina to Laity*, p. 675.

6. A certain ascetic in the deep desert saw, from a high rock, green grass below; and he saw a man grazing on the grass like an animal. The ascetic approached him stealthily and caught the man. He was old and completely naked. Unable to stand the smell of man, he broke loose and quickly ran off. The brother chased after him, shouting: "It is for the sake of God that I am after you, wait for me." The Elder replied: "And I am running away from you for the sake of the same God." Then he advised the brother: "Run away from men and you will attain salvation." Here is an example of self-renunciation, brought to the extreme. *Ancient Patericon*, XX, II, p. 455.

See Florovsky, *Byzantine Fathers of the 5th to 8th Centuries*, p. 143.

ST. SABBAS THE SANCTIFIED

A contemporary icon depicting Saints associated with St. Sabbas' Monastery.

life as an anchorite, dedicating it to a solitary study of his soul. No one's instructions are imbued with a more profound psychological content than are his homilies. Having ascended through the degrees of the spiritual contemplative life himself, St. Isaac based his instructions concerning lofty contemplation on his own profound experience.

The Moslem invasion in the 7th century delivered a blow to monasticism. The Arabs conquered Syria in 636, Palestine in 637 and Egypt in 640. Monasticism could not flourish during Moslem rule in these lands. Abiza, the ruler of Egypt, issued a decree prohibiting people from becoming monastics. In 715 he repeated the decree, and monks were subjected to torture. When three Patriarchates — those of Antioch, Jerusalem and Alexandria — were cut off from the Byzantine Church during the Moslem rule, the entire monastic life concentrated mainly in the Patriarchate of Constantinople. Byzantium at that time was covered with monasteries; it was like a monastic kingdom. There were monasteries for men, for women, and mixed monasteries.[7] As to their way of life, there were coenobitic and idiorhythmic monasteries. Many monks were desert-dwellers (anchorites, hermits) and they lived in individual cells and sketes attached to lavras. They followed the Rules established by Sts. Pachomius and Basil the Great; these Rules formed the basis of the Rules of Sts. Sabbas the Sanctified, Athanasius of Mount Athos, Theodore the Studite, and others.

Byzantine monasticism victoriously carried Orthodoxy on its shoulders during the iconoclastic war which arose during the reign of Leo the Isaurian (717-741), who wanted to reform the Church in the interests of the state and to subject the Church to the state completely.

In the 9th century, monastic eldership was officially recognized by the Church and also acquired external influence and significance.

This happened due to the steadfastness and firmness of the monks during their persecution. In connection with these events, the name of **St. Theodore the Studite** (†826), came into the light. From 798 he was the Abbot of the monastery of Studium, founded in the 5th century by the Roman nobleman Studios. St. Theodore took up the defense of icons, and suffered torture and imprisonment until the end of the iconoclastic persecution. St. Theodore compiled the famous Studite Rule, which was adopted in Russia when the Kiev Monastery of the Caves was founded. St. Theodore is well known as a Church writer and compiler of Church hymns.

The focal point of monasticism at the end of the 10th century was **St. Simeon the New Theologian** (†1032). His theology formed the basis for the de-

---

7. "Mixed monasteries" were commonly for elderly people on pensions, and were based on an idiorhythmic principle (*editor*).

velopment of the hesychast teaching. In his youth he was brought up near the imperial court; later he joined the Studite Monastery, where he was under the guidance of Elder Simeon the Reverent, and observed strict rules of fasting. From there he moved to St. Mamas' Monastery. During his ordination to the priesthood, the light of the Spirit of God visibly descended upon him. Later he became an abbot. St. Simeon was an inspired writer, concentrating on the topics of prayer and contemplation. He became one of the few saints upon whom the Church bestowed the designation of Theologian.

In the history of Mt. Athos, chronologically the anchoretic type of monasticism appeared first, then coenobitic life. The latter, however, is regarded as a type of life suited for beginners, and preliminary to the anchoretic life.

The first known recluse and hesychastic ascetic of Mt. Athos was St. Peter the Athonite (†734); and up to the 9th century only this type of monasticism (anchoretic) existed on Mt. Athos.

In the 10th century, however, due to the decline of the anchoretic life, St. Athanasius the Athonite (born 930) established a coenobitic lavra on Mt. Athos. Thus began the struggle between the two views on asceticism. This struggle continued for a few centuries and, as a result, it weakened the spiritual activity of the monks. This weakening, however, was caused not so much by the internal disagreement as by external blows and ravages of Mt. Athos. In 1204 Mt. Athos was seized by the Latins (the 4th crusade). Pope Innocent III annexed the entire Athos Peninsula to his personal estate, and he sent his representative there with instructions to convert everyone to Roman Catholicism. This was the beginning of a reign of cruel terrorism. The Bulgarian King John Asen II defeated the Latins near Adrianopolis, thus freeing the Holy Mountain, but not for long. In 1267 Emperor Michael Paleologus, wishing to receive assistance from the Pope in his fight against the Ottoman Turks, agreed to accept the union of Rome and Constantinople. In October of 1267, Roman Catholics and Byzantine apostates appeared on Mt. Athos and resumed persecution of the Orthodox monks. The lavra of St. Athanasius alone gave itself over for the sake of money. Other monasteries, like Zographou, Iveron and Vatopedi, remained faithful to Orthodoxy. The Zographou monks were burned, those of Vatopedi were hanged, and those of Iveron were thrown into the sea. Russian and Serbian monasteries were burned. Four hundred cart-loads of Athonite sacred objects and literary treasures were taken to the West. In 1313 Mt. Athos was delivered from the Latins. All these ravages unfavorably affected the inner life of the Athonites, but their spiritual activity was not lost permanently. When in the 14th century St. Gregory of Sinai (†1346) came to Mt. Athos, he addressed the ascetics "well adorned with active virtues" with the question: "Do you practice inward prayer, sobriety

ST. ATHANASIUS THE ATHONITE (THE COENOBIARCH)
A fresco in the Great Lavra, Mt. Athos.

THE MONASTERY OF DIONYSIOU ON MT. ATHOS
as it looks today.

PILLARS OF MONASTICISM
Left to right: St. Athanasius the Athonite, St. Simeon of Serbia,
St. Theodore Studite, St. Onuphrius the Great, St. Macarius the Great,
St. John of Rila, and St. John Cassian the Roman.

A fresco from the refectory of Holy Trinity Monastery, Jordanville.

and watchfulness of the mind?" They replied that they did not even know what these words meant. Having inspected the Holy Mountain, he settled finally in the skete of Magula, situated near the Philotheou Monastery, and there he found three monks who were engaged "not only in inward prayer, but also in contemplation."[8]

In the 13th and 14th centuries there occurred a new spiritual renaissance of the entire East. Mt. Athos became one of the spiritual centers. Professor Syrkou points out that Mt. Athos was of great significance in the inner life of southeastern Europe, particularly in the spheres of the enlightenment and preservation of pure Orthodoxy in Byzantium and among the Slavs. At that time Mt. Athos was the stronghold of Orthodox asceticism and of the Orthodox Faith itself. Among the Athonites there were many great men adorned with lofty ascetic labors and virtues; there were many erudite men of profound knowledge in contemporary sciences. They flocked to Mt. Athos from everywhere, from all parts of the Orthodox and heterodox worlds. From ancient times, Mt. Athos was a populous monastic republic which owned land in various places on the Balkan Peninsula. Emperor Michael Paleologus, in the *chrysobul*[9] given to St. Athanasius' Lavra in 1257, called Mt. Athos "a holy Mount, beloved by God and chosen to be His abode." Some of the Athonite ascetics did not regard scholarly work as being of primary importance, but the majority of them were obviously bibliophiles, judging by the huge libraries of some Athonite monasteries. A great ascetic or a great scholar would be a luminary to the entire Greek and Slavic world and would attract many disciples. Such great elders would instruct these disciples not only in inward prayer, but also in other spiritual matters or sciences, since Mt. Athos would render all the means possible towards this end. Mt. Athos kept and preserved the purity of Orthodox teaching and the inviolability of Church books. Among the spiritual leaders of the 14th century were St. Gregory of Sinai — who, while on Mt. Athos, promoted and defined the rule of silent mental prayer — his friend St. Maximus of Kapsokalyvia, St. Gregory Palamas and several patriarchs of Constantinople.[10]

---

8. *Athonite Patericon*, Vol. I, p. 388. Also, Syrkou, *A History of The Correction of Books in Bulgaria*, Vol. I, p. 66.

9. *Chrysobul*: a document with a golden seal issued by government authorities *(editor)*.

10. Syrkou, *A History of the Correction of Books in Bulgaria*, pp. 55-60.

KAROULIA, MT. ATHOS
where hesychasts have dwelt for centuries.

Chapter Three

HESYCHASM

THUS, THE 14TH CENTURY was remarkable for a new spiritual renaissance in the East. This renaissance found its expression in hesychasm, which subsequently caused the well-known and lengthy "hesychast" disputes, where clashed the Eastern and Western world-views. The controversy generated great agitation in the political life of Byzantium. It ended with the implicit triumph of hesychasm; and the Orthodox Church formally adopted the doctrine of Divine Energies. What is the origin of hesychasm and what is its essence?

It all began with the arrival in Byzantium of Barlaam, a Calabrian monk, during the first years of the reign of Emperor Andronicus the Younger (reigned 1328-1341). Barlaam began to propagate the teaching of Abelard, which maintained that truth may be considered as truth only when proven by reason exclusively. He preached a teaching in addition to rationalism, that of Thomas Aquinas, which expressed the idea that God was wholly essence and that in Him essence and action were indistinguishable. All manifestations of Divinity were to be considered as created, even the gifts of the Holy Spirit.

Contrary to this view, St. Gregory Palamas and his Athonite co-strugglers taught and proved by their lives that it was not by way of philosophical reasoning, but through constant purification of the soul, perfect stillness of feelings and thoughts, unceasing practice in theology and mental prayer or "mental activity" that man could attain enlightenment from above. However, man cannot behold the Essence of Divinity, which dwells in "inaccessible light" and is therefore beyond the reach of our limited created nature, but only the Divine Energies

($\epsilon\nu\epsilon\rho\gamma\epsilon\iota\alpha$), describable as active motion. The word was used in this sense by Aristotle. "The emanation of God's Essence is usually revealed to hesychasts in the form of light, which can sometimes be seen also with bodily eyes."[1]

The collision between the Western and Orthodox world-views gave rise to many philosophic arguments and to discussions in the Church Councils. In this battle, the place of primary significance belonged to St. Gregory Palamas. His achievement consisted not only of the fact that he bore on his shoulders the heavy burden of the struggle for hesychasm, but also that he expressed and defined the mystical experiences of the hesychasts in clear and precise philosophical concepts congenial to the Orthodox Church. His defense of hesychasm finally resulted in the formal adoption of hesychast theology in the Church at the Council of 1352.

We should now pause to examine the essence of hesychasm.

Hesychasm is an old concept of the Eastern Church, and denotes an ascetic practice associated with the anchoretic way of life and stillness ($\dot{\eta}\sigma\upsilon\chi\acute{\iota}\alpha$ — stillness). In the early Byzantine period, hesychasm denoted the ascetic endeavor of a solitary desert-dweller (hermit). In the later Byzantine period, hesychasts were known as monks who devoted themselves to absolute silence, holy repose, inner spiritual concentration and unceasing "mental" prayer ($\nu o \epsilon \rho \acute{\alpha} \; \pi \rho o \sigma \epsilon \upsilon \chi \acute{\eta}$). This practice eventually led to a particular inexplicable state of blessedness, to the vision of a certain heavenly Light which is not of this world, uncreated and similar to the Light which surrounded the Savior on Mt. Tabor. Such a type of hesychasm was formed in the 14th century. Ancient asceticism contributed greatly towards the emergence of this spiritual type.

St. Simeon the New Theologian of the 11th century is usually considered the father of hesychasm. He was the first to clearly develop the teaching on the vision of God. However, "hesychasm" was not something entirely new. It began alongside the emergence of monasticism. "Mental prayer," as the means facilitating hesychia or stillness, was not an invention of 11th-century innovators. Long before that time, the founders of monasticism taught unceasing prayer as the means to strengthen "inward attention" and achieve sobriety of the heart.

Hierarch Porphyrius Uspensky found, in the libraries of Mt. Athos, 10th-15th-century anthologies with selections from ancient Patericons about prayer and inward activity. These prove that the sources of hesychasm stem from St. Anthony the Great (3rd century), St. Macarius the Great (4th century), St. John of the Ladder (6th century), etc. Already in his time, Abba Anthony taught about stillness: "Let us be men of silence and hesychasts." He instructed

---

1. *Manual for Clergy* (Kiev, 1915), p. 570.

Blessed Theodora on the necessity of becoming quiet and keeping silence, of sitting in her cell and recollecting the mind within herself. Blessed Theodora said: "Rest from cares, silence, and the innermost soaring of the mind constitute unceasing prayer: Lord Jesus Christ, Son of God, help me."[2] The Jesus Prayer is often mentioned in the *Lausiac History* and other anthologies. The first noted hesychast-hermit on Mt. Athos was St. Peter the Athonite, who was actually the founder of hesychasm there. He had a number of followers. Mt. Athos had a remarkable hesychast center, a "hesychasterion" — "a place of stillness," later called Magula — which was built by a Georgian, Sabbas Khald, between the Iveron and the Philotheou Monasteries during the reign of Emperor Basil the Macedonian, at the end of the 9th century.

Hesychast ideology goes back to the mystical teaching of the ancient Christian Church. Of great significance was **St. Dionysius the Areopagite. St. Maximus the Confessor** (†662) introduced and adopted Dionysian mysticism into the Church. He searched for ways beyond reason and sense to attain closeness with Divinity. Both St. Dionysius and St. Maximus spoke of the inexpressible light which envelopes a man contemplating Divinity. The true spiritual founding father of Athonite hesychasts, however, was St. Simeon the New Theologian, the greatest mystic at the turn of the millenium, who clearly showed that the highest objective of ascetic endeavors was to behold the Divine Light. The main purpose of man's life was moral enlightenment through entering within oneself and spiritual concentration.

It is well known that the hesychast doctrine identifies the light perceived by some ascetics with the Light of Mt. Tabor which enveloped Christ during His Transfiguration. On these grounds, the opinion was formed that the doctrine of light was an innovation introduced by the 14th century hesychasts. However, the teaching on light had existed from the beginning of monasticism, while St. Gregory Palamas was only the first to refer to the Light of Mt. Tabor in his defense against opponents. At the time of the controversy, the hesychast teaching had already been completely formed. The only new thing which surfaced during these famous disputes, when the entire teaching of hesychasm was discussed, was the question of the physical method employed by ascetics during prayer in order to enhance concentration and intensify attention.[3] The period wherein this method originated cannot be precisely established. It was practiced from ancient times, and was passed down orally. Meanwhile, the moment in Church history arrived when an open discussion of the entire doctrine of hesychasm had become

2. Archimandrite Cyprian, *Anthropology of St. Gregory Palamas*, p. 65.
3. A particular bodily posture, control of the breathing so as to keep time with the recitation of the prayer, and centering attention in the upper part of the heart.

necessary in order that its formal and legitimate right to exist be acknowledged. Bishop Porphyrius Uspensky says: "The entire doctrine of Athonite hesychasts was not at all new to the 14th century. No. It had been treasured not only on Mt. Athos, but wherever there were men of silence . . . and it never embarrassed Christian society. But when it was discovered by the Calabrian monk Barlaam, the Church of Constantinople, usually sensitive to popular subjects of discussion, brought it out at the Councils." Archimandrite Cyprian explains: "It was precisely for this reason that in the Council decisions — the resolutions of 1341 and subsequent years — the Church came forward with a definite statement that the hesychast doctrine was in keeping with the spirit of Church tradition and with monastic experience."[4]

Hesychasm was conservative by nature and preserved traditions. The teaching on mental prayer was systematized and expounded by St. Gregory of Sinai on the precise basis of patristic teaching. "We know," continues Archimandrite Cyprian, "with what bitterness the Athonite hesychasts were attacked by Barlaam, Grigora and Acyndinus, and how many accusations were cast against St. Gregory Palamas. His name never left the lips of his contemporaries and abounded in statements of the Councils. But if St. Gregory of Sinai was the founder of hesychasm, why is there no mention of his name in any of the synodal or Athonite resolutions? It would have been natural to attack him as an innovator. The fact is, however, that hesychia and mental prayer are not innovations of the 14th century. . . . "[5]

Let us look at what constitutes the hesychast teaching. It is summarized by the following:

1. God's Essence (ουσία) must be distinguished from His manifestations (Energies) (ενέργεια).

2. Divine Energy is uncreated, as is God's Divine Essence.

3. The difference between the Essence and the manifestation of Divinity does not bring about any complication in the concept of God.

4. The Holy Fathers apply the word "Divinity" not only to the Essence of God, but also to His Energies.

5. According to the Holy Fathers, the essence is superior to its manifestation, as the cause is superior to its effect.

6. God's presence transcends the created world (is beyond the world), and is therefore inaccessible to the comprehension of man, who may behold God only in His manifestations — His grace (χάρις), power (δύναμις), love, wisdom, etc.

4. Archimandrite Cyprian, *Anthropology of St. Gregory Palamas*, p. 65.
5. *Ibid.*, p. 63.

MOUNT SINAI
The Monastery of St. Catherine, dedicated to the Transfiguration,
where lived Saints John Climacus and Gregory of Sinai.

The light of Mt. Tabor that radiated from the Lord during His Transfiguration is neither created light nor the Essence of God (ουσία). It is the grace-bestowing emanation of Divinity, the uncreated and eternal light, accessible to bodily perception, one of the forms of energy, always emanating from the very Essence of God.[6]

---

6. G. A. Ostrogradsky, "Athonite Hesychasts and Their Opponents," in *Transactions of the Russian Scientific Institute*, no. 5 (Belgrade, 1931), pp. 353-355.

ST. GREGORY OF SINAI

Icon by Photios Kontoglou.

Chapter Four

SAINTS GREGORY OF SINAI
AND GREGORY PALAMAS

SAINTS GREGORY OF SINAI AND GREGORY PALAMAS became prominent on Mt. Athos during the golden age of hesychasm.

St. Gregory of Sinai (†1346)[1] was born in the 60's of the 13th century in Asia Minor. He received an excellent education. In his youth he was captured by the Turks. After being ransomed, he became a monk and spent some time in the Monastery of St. Catherine on Mt. Sinai. Hence, he is known as St. Gregory of Sinai. As he was returning from a pilgrimage to Jerusalem, he stopped on the island of Crete, where he met the hermit Elder Arsenius, who taught him mental prayer. Subsequently he settled on Mt. Athos, where he spent time in lofty spiritual ascetic endeavors. Around him gathered disciples, one more remarkable than the other. He instructed them in mental activity. Besides his disciples, he taught everyone who came to see him. Thus, not only was he renowned on Mt. Athos, having influence and respect among Athonite brothers in general, but "almost everyone considered it a great misfortune not to have visited him and been vouchsafed to hear his teachings." These words were said by his biographer, Patriarch Callistus, who added that the power of St. Gregory's teaching left a deep impression on people due to its evocativeness. These people said: "When St. Gregory expounded about purity of the soul and how a man may become God through grace, then in our souls would awaken a kind of divine, irrepres-

---

1. Commemorated August 8.

sible longing for virtue and limitless love for God." "This makes it obvious," says Professor P. A. Syrkou, "that St. Gregory was a strong individual, highly endowed with the qualities of soul which made him an excellent preacher and disseminator of his ideas, inspiring in his listeners faith in this idea, because he himself was wholly imbued with it. This exalted ascetic 'compelled both the desert-dwellers and coenobites, and everyone else, to practice mental prayer and the guarding of the mind,' his hagiographer added. The turbulent spirit of the time compelled him to move out to Paroria in Thrace, bordering Bulgaria. Hence, many Bulgarian monks began to flock around him. Thus, in a note added to the handwritten codex of his writings we read: ' . . . He was the first to instruct Bulgarians and Serbs in inward mental activity according to the tradition and art of the ancient Fathers.' St. Gregory's teaching on the principles of an austere ascetic life was disseminated not only among the Greeks, Bulgarians and Serbs, but also in more remote regions, if not directly by him, at least through his numerous disciples, who played an outstanding role in the Church history of southeastern Europe during the 14th century."[2]

St. Gregory formulated the general teaching on hesychia. His main work of 150 chapters is a treatise on mental prayer.

St. Gregory Palamas (†1360)[3] was also born in Asia Minor (probably in the last decade of the 13th century). He received a splendid education at the imperial court. Both of his teachers, secular and spiritual, instructed him in his youth in the practice of inward spiritual activity; and at the age of twenty, St. Gregory chose the monastic path. First he lived on Mt. Athos in St. Athanasius' Lavra, and later in the Glossia Skete, where he spent ten years in unceasing prayer, weeping, fasting and vigils. The Turkish invasion forced him to leave Mt. Athos. He went to Thessalonica, where he was ordained priest. Here again he led the life of an anchorite with twelve other brothers, communicating with them once a week. "At that time he was slightly over thirty years of age, and his perfect health and bodily strength did not fail him. But in order to subject his body in all its aspects to the spirit, he observed an extremely austere way of life which was difficult for his fleshly thinking and for his will. This proved to be of benefit to his brothers; they were edified by such an exalted model of monastic perfection." Indeed, according to his Life, where reference is made to his spiritual states, St. Gregory must have exercised great influence upon his monastic brothers. "It often happened that he would immerse himself in profound stillness, and tears would stream from his eyes. But whenever he opened his lips to speak, his listeners were sincerely moved in heart, became enthused and wept. In the hours fol-

---

2. Syrkou, *A History of the Correction of Books in Bulgaria*, pp. 75 and 62.
3. Commemorated November 14 and on the second Sunday of Great Lent.

lowing his periods of reclusion, and particularly after Liturgy, his face was glorious to behold, with wondrous divine light playing upon his features. During his life there, St. Gregory made friends with a simple Elder and man of silence, Job. Once, as the Elder was listening to St. Gregory's idea that not only ascetics but all Christians should pray without ceasing, according to apostolic command, he voiced his disagreement, objecting that unceasing prayer is the duty of monastics, not laymen. Gregory, who disliked verbosity, did not say anything in reply. But as soon as Elder Job returned to his cell and began to pray, an angel revealed to him that every Christian is obliged to pray, and that Gregory had spoken the truth."[4]

Subsequently, St. Gregory was elected Abbot of Esphigmenou Monastery, where he worked many miracles, such as turning fruitless olive trees and vines into fruit-bearing ones, filling empty containers with oil, etc. Later he entered a period of his life filled with struggles against the heretics Barlaam and Acyndinus. First he succeeded in disgracing them at the Council of 1341.[5] Later, however, as a result of intrigues on the part of the heretics, a new Council was convened in which the opponents scored a victory, while St. Gregory was thrown into a dark prison. He was released from the prison thanks to the intercession of the Empress. Then he was consecrated Bishop of Thessalonica, but his new flock rejected him and he returned to Mt. Athos. The Serbian King Stephan Dushan failed to persuade him to accept the chair of Metropolitan of Bulgaria. But even on Mt. Athos St. Gregory could not find rest, and he returned to Constantinople and settled on the island of Lemnos. Finally, the flock of Thessalonica requested his return and received him with great honor. St. Gregory once again was destined to endure heavy trials: he was captured by the Turks, who tortured him almost to death. He was ransomed by the Bulgarians. During the last three years of his life, St. Gregory worked many miracles. On November 13 (the day of St. Gregory's commemoration), St. John Chrysostom appeared to him and summoned him as a friend to come and share with him the peace of the mansions of Paradise. The next day St. Gregory died. "Higher, higher, towards the Light," were his last words.

The glorious blossoming of Mt. Athos left its traces in many spiritual writers, such as Patriarch Callistus of Constantinople, his friend Ignatius (both called Xanthopoulos), Callistus Kataphagiotes, Archbishop Simeon of Thessalonica, Monk Nicephorus, and Patriarch Philotheus of Constantinople. They continued developing the views of St. Gregory of Sinai, particularly concentrating on

---

4. Syrkou, *A History of the Correction of Books in Bulgaria*, pp. 83-84.
5. Later the Barlaam heresy was exposed and its adherents anathematized at the Councils of 1347, 1351, 1352, and 1368 (already after the death of St. Gregory).

ST. PAISIUS VELICHKOVSKY

spiritual prayer. Later ensued another period of decline. It may be assumed that it was caused by the general disastrous situation on Mt. Athos under the Turkish rule (1371). This rule, however, was incomparably less cruel than the Latin domination. The Athonites had to pay tribute, and Mt. Athos was inaccessible to pilgrims because of the wars. Russia was the only sponsor of Mt. Athos during the 16th-18th centuries. On more than fifty occasions, delegations of Athonite monks came to Russia to collect funds, and each time they returned with gold and other treasures. The second half of the 18th century witnessed a rebirth of hesychasm. A Greek monk, St. Nicodemus of the Holy Mountain (1747-1809), delved deeply into patristic writings, which he systematized in the course of many decades. He was particularly meticulous in his treatment of St. Gregory of Sinai and other hesychasts. His works were printed in the Greek language in Venice and published in 1782 under the title of *The Philokalia*. Elder Paisius Velichkovsky (1722-1794) translated this publication into Slavonic (called *Dobrotolubie*). This Slavonic-Russian *Philokalia*, reviewed at the Academy of St. Alexander Nevsky and in the Holy Trinity Lavra, was published in Moscow in 1793 through the efforts of Metropolitan Gabriel of St. Petersburg and Novgorod.

For more help on the path of spiritual struggle:

THE SPIRITUAL LIFE is a primer to guide the soul to that realm of the Spirit into which "the wisdom of this world does not penetrate." Written by a master of the Prayer of the Heart, this book contains instructions which will help one attune the soul to be in harmony with the voice of God, echoing in the instrument of the heart.

320 pages, paperback, illustrated, $12.95. Please add 10% postage.
Order from: St. Paisius Abbey, P. O. Box 130, Forestville, CA 95436

Silence
&
Solitude

Mystical Literature
from the Christian East

St. Herman Press

ST. HERMAN OF ALASKA BROTHERHOOD

For three decades, the St. Herman Brotherhood has been publishing works of traditional Christian spirituality.

Write for our free 80-page catalogue, featuring sixty titles of published and forthcoming books and magazines.

St. Herman Press
10 Beegum Gorge Road
P. O. Box 70, Dept. ACQ
Platina, CA 96076